OSPREY AIRCRAFT OF THE ACES • 86

P-36 Hawk Aces of World War 2

SERIES EDITOR: TONY HOLMES

OSPREY AIRCRAFT OF THE ACES • 86

P-36 Hawk Aces of World War 2

Lionel Persyn, Kari Stenman
and Andrew Thomas

OSPREY
PUBLISHING

Front Cover
Shortly after 0800 hrs on Sunday, 7 December 1941, the first Japanese bombs struck Wheeler Field, on the Hawaiian island of Oahu, as the devastating attack on Pearl Harbor began. A number of pilots headed by car to the auxiliary airfield at Haleiwa, some 15 miles away, where a small number of P-40Bs and P-36As had been detached for gunnery qualification training – the latter were armed with just a single nose-mounted 0.30-in machine gun. The first pilots to arrive grabbed two available P-40s, leaving the four P-36s for the others. Among the latter was 19-year-old 2Lt Harry W Brown of the 15th Pursuit Group's 47th Pursuit Squadron, who jumped into his own P-36, which carried a white '2' on either side of its fin.

Taking off at 0830 hrs, he headed for nearby Bellows Field. As he approached the base, Brown and another P-36 pilot (possibly 2Lt Bob Rogers) dived on a Japanese aircraft that quickly disappeared into cloud. He also lost sight of the second Hawk at this time too. Flying over Kaneohe Point, Brown spotted three aircraft. As he closed in on them, he realised that it was a pair of Japanese aircraft (B5N 'Kate' torpedo-bombers) bearing down on the tail of his erstwhile companion, 2Lt Bob Rogers. Brown recalled;

'They were slightly below me, and I dove toward the second one. He snap-turned inside me, leaving me almost on the tail of the first one. He made a mistake! He tried to turn away from me and, of course, flew right through my line of fire. I wasn't more than 10-15 ft behind him, and I couldn't have missed. I saw the rear gunner crumple and the left wing begin to burn, so I snapped to the right and climbed to set myself up for another pass. I saw the aeroplane I had hit go into the water almost vertically.'

Rogers' P-36 had been damaged by the 'Kates', and he was forced to land. As Brown turned to port in search of the second B5N, he was suddenly confronted by a dozen others immediately in front of him – he flew right through the formation! Brown dived on a straggler, only to discover that it was another P-36. Not for the first time that day the radial-engined Curtiss had been mistaken for the enemy. The USAAC fighter attacked one of the 'Kates' and then broke off, its pilot having exhausted his ammunition. Brown then made three firing passes before his guns also fell silent;

'I know I inflicted heavy damage on my first pass. I saw the pilot's canopy shatter and the engine take some hits. The last time I saw him, he was headed out over Kaena Point in the general direction of Kauai, trailing a column of black smoke and rapidly losing altitude.'

He then returned to Haleiwa where, much to his crew chief's amusement, Brown realised that he was still wearing his pyjama top and tuxedo trousers from the previous night's celebrations! Harry Brown subsequently flew an additional sortie that same day, and two years later his second victim was upgraded from 'probable' to destroyed. The two B5Ns (originally credited as D3A 'Val' dive-bombers) were his first steps to acedom, which he achieved flying P-38s with the 475th Fighter Group over New Guinea in 1943 (*Cover artwork by Mark Postlethwaite*)

First published in Great Britain in 2009 by Osprey Publishing
Midland House, West Way, Botley, Oxford, OX2 0PH
443 Park Avenue South, New York, NY, 10016, USA
E-mail: info@ospreypublishing.com

© 2009 Osprey Publishing Limited

Print ISBN: 978 1 84603 409 1
PDF e-book ISBN: 978 1 84603 862 4

Edited by Tony Holmes
Page design by Tony Truscott
Cover Artwork by Mark Postlethwaite
Aircraft Profiles by Chris Davey
Scale Drawings by Mark Styling
Index by Alan Thatcher
Printed and bound in China by Bookbuilders

09 10 11 12 13   10 9 8 7 6 5 4 3 2 1

For a catalogue of all books published by Osprey please contact:
NORTH AMERICA
Osprey Direct, C/o Random House Distribution Center,
400 Hahn Road, Westminster, MD 21157
E-mail: uscustomerservice@ospreypublishing.com

ALL OTHER REGIONS
Osprey Direct, The Book Service Ltd, Distribution Centre, Colchester Road, Frating Green, Colchester, Essex, CO7 7DW, UK
E-mail: customerservice@ospreypublishing.com
www.ospreypublishing.com

CONTENTS

GENESIS

Twenty-one years after the guns had fallen silent over the muddy trenches of the Western Front, the fighters of the French *l'Armee de l'Air* were once again patrolling the border on the lookout for a German enemy. Following the invasion of Poland on 1 September 1939, both Britain and France honoured their treaty obligations and on the 3rd found themselves once more at war with Germany.

Soon after dawn on 8 September, six radial-engined French fighters of *Groupe de Chasse* (GC) II/4, led by Adj Chef Robert Cruchant, were patrolling over the Landau-Saargemund area when they came under sustained anti-aircraft fire. Some 30 minutes later, the French patrol was attacked by a four Bf 109Es from I./JG 53, led by the experienced Oberleutnant Werner Mölders, who was the ranking German ace of the Spanish Civil War. Mölders' formation attacked the leading trio in the French formation, but without success, upon which the eager French pilots turned into the attackers.

A brief dogfight duly commenced, following which the 'Emils' dived away and two were reported by the French pilots as having come down behind German lines – these successes were later confirmed. Adj Pierre Villey, Sgt Chef Antoine Casenobe and Adj Chef Robert Cruchant were credited with two destroyed between them. For the former pair, it was also their first steps to acedom. Upon his return to base, Cruchant wrote;

'Over Winden, the monotony of the sortie was broken by heavy flak – we made it back to our lines harassed by some well-aimed height-adjusted salvoes. Just after, without warning, we were jumped by Messerschmitts all guns blazing. Hauling back hard on our sticks, we reared up like vipers, causing the '109s to overshoot. Casenobe unleashed a burst from long range at the first enemy machine that had opened up on me. I came out of my steep bank turn to see a '109 pass in front of me. Overhead, Casenobe fell on him and chased him all the way down to 1500 m, spraying copious fire, at which height the Messerschmitt rolled over onto its back.

'Villey was seen grappling with three '109s. Twisting and turning, he got in behind one and filled it with lead, only easing up to shake off another adversary that had got on his tail. As for myself – the pigeon turned mother hen – I attempted to go to the aid of Villey and Casenobe, but the bastards fell on me again and wouldn't let go. I threw my kite into some wild manoeuvres each time they opened up, and I even caught one when I turned and faced him. Front three-quarters, aim, fire . . . gotcha! I managed to scare off the other '109 pilot that tried to assist his comrade.'

In fact only Mölders' aircraft had been badly hit, forcing him down into an open meadow near Birkenfeld, some distance short of his base at Wiesbaden. The Messerschmitt somersaulted and the ace suffered a painful injury to his back, resulting in a brief period of recuperation.

The victorious pilots had not been flying a French aircraft, however, but an elegant American design in the form of the Curtiss Hawk 75A, which they thus blooded in combat. The fighter had started to reach

Three of the five pilots from GC II/4 'Red Devils' that engaged in the Hawk 75's first successful combat pose in front of a Curtiss fighter shortly after the 8 September 1939 clash. They are, from left to right, Adj Pierre Villey, Sgt Chef Antoine Casenobe and Sgt Francois Dietrich. Both Villey and Casenobe subsequently became aces, although the former was ultimately killed in action on 25 May 1940 (*J Prott*)

French units in substantial numbers earlier in the year.

On his return on 20 September, Mölders swiftly gained revenge when he shot down Sgt Quéguiner's Hawk 75 for his first kill in World War 2. The GC II/5 pilot baled out. Squadronmate Sgt André Legrand evened up the score when he downed Unteroffizier Winkler's 'Emil'. Mölders described his victory thus;

'I took off with my *schwarm* at 1427 hrs to intercept six enemy monoplanes reported south of Trier. As the *schwarm* overflew the River Saar near Merzig at 4500 metres, six machines were sighted south of Contz at 5000 metres. I climbed above the enemy in a wide curve to the north and carried out a surprise attack on the rearmost machine. I opened fire form approximately 50 metres, whereupon the Curtiss began to fishtail. After a further lengthy burst, smoke came out of the machine and individual pieces flew off it. It then tipped forward into a dive and I lost sight of it, as I had to defend myself against other opponents newly arriving on the scene.'

Despite having acquitted itself well in these early clashes, the reality was that the little Curtiss fighter was already outclassed by the leading British and German designs. Nevertheless, the duels of the 'Phoney War' marked the start of a five-year combat career for the American fighter, during which it was to see action in the colours of a number of nations, fighting both for and against the Allies.

The Hawk 75's first victim was no less a pilot than leading Spanish Civil War ace Oberleutnant Werner Mölders of I./JG 51, who was forced down after a brief clash with GC II/4 on 8 September 1939. Despite suffering a painful back injury, Mölders survived this incident and was back in the cockpit within a fortnight. On 20 September he exacted his revenge when he downed a Hawk 75 from GC II/5 – the first example of the Curtiss fighter to be lost in combat (*via John Weal*)

NEW FIGHTER

In 1934 the US Army had issued a specification for a new all-metal, low wing fighter capable of 300 mph. Among those that responded was the design team of the Curtiss-Wright Company's Airplane Division, led by Donovan R Berlin. It offered the Model 75 as a replacement for the USAAC's elderly P-26 fighters. However, during the fly-off competition in April 1936, engine problems with the Model 75 allowed the Seversky P-35 to win. Nonetheless, an order for three YIP-36s was placed, and in a further competition the following year the Curtiss design won. On 7 July 1937 the US Army contracted the company to build 210 P-36As – the largest single aircraft order placed with a US manufacturer since 1918.

The 1st Pursuit Group (PG), comprising the 17th, 27th and 94th Pursuit Sqns (PSs), at Selfridge Field, in Michigan, was the first to begin re-equipment. However, skin buckling, cracking engine exhausts and other problems meant that only a handful were regularly available. The 94th PS was the only unit to receive P-36s in 1938, with the 27th being issued with a small number in early 1939. Neither unit ever managed a full complement of P-36s, and the 17th never received a single one!

In spite of these early problems, during the course of 1939 the 8th PG (33rd, 35th and 36th PSs) at Langley Field, Virginia, was equipped with P-36s. One of the pilots serving with the 36th PS was 2Lt Hubert Zemke,

who subsequently became a leading ace and fighter leader with the Eighth Air Force in Europe. He recalled, 'With the P-36 we had a fighter that could just about catch the B-17s of the 2nd BG, but it was lacking performance compared to what we heard about the latest European fighters.'

The 20th PG (55th, 77th and 79th PSs) also re-equipped, although by 1940 the USAAC recognised that the P-36 was obsolescent. Indeed, during 1941 the fighter was largely supplanted in frontline service by such types as the Bell P-39 and its lineal successor, the Curtiss P-40. Although it remained in limited service overseas, in the US most P-36s had been passed on to training units by the time of the attack on Pearl Harbor.

Other P-36s were transferred to the 16th PG (24th, 29th and 43rd PSs) and 32nd PG (51st, 52nd and 53rd PSs), both of which were based at Albrook Field in the Panama Canal Zone. Elsewhere, during February 1941, 20 P-36s were delivered to Alaska, where they were used by the 18th PS at Elmendorf Field, near Anchorage. Other P-36s arrived in Hawaii from San Diego aboard the carrier USS *Enterprise* for use by the 18th PG (78th PS) and the newly formed 15th PG (45th, 46th and 47th PSs) at Wheeler Field, Hawaii. It was aircraft of the latter group that were destined to be the only P-36s to see combat in US colours. Serving with the 15th PG was future Eighth Air Force ace 2Lt Francis Gabreski;

'I was assigned to the 45th PS of the 15th PG. I was stepping up to the P-36 and P-40. My squadron commander was Capt Aaron Tyer. When it came to flight leaders, I had a dandy – 1Lt Woody Wilmot. I would say Woody had more to do with me becoming a successful fighter pilot than anyone. I flew the P-36 a lot in Hawaii. The P-36 was about 1500 lbs lighter than the P-40, which made it a joy to fly. It had a short nose with a radial engine that pumped out enough power to give you full control during all the aerobatic manoeuvres, and it was responsive to the flight controls. The 45th was equipped with a mixed complement of P-36s and P-40s, so we flew whatever type was available on any given day.'

OVERSEAS SALES

By the late 1930s, Europe was in the grip of a massive re-armament programme by potential protagonists, and it was natural that the export

In July 1937, Curtiss secured the largest single aircraft order placed with an American manufacturer since 1918 when the US Army contracted it to build 210 P-36 Hawks. By the time the first examples reached the 1st PG in April 1938, its performance was, at best, relatively mediocre when compared with fighter designs entering service with air arms in Europe. Nevertheless, the P-36 was blessed with unmatched manoeuvrability. This particular example was assigned to the 55th PS/20th PG at Barksdale Field, in Louisiana, in 1940 (*ww2images*)

version of the latest US fighter should be examined by several nations. When offered for overseas sale, the P-36 was marketed by Curtiss as the Hawk 75, and the aircraft duly won sizeable orders that resulted in it seeing widespread service across the globe.

Even as it entered US service, the P-36 was being evaluated for possible use by the *l'Armee de l'Air*, resulting in large orders being placed. The first Hawk 75A-1 reached France in late February 1939, and further deliveries resulted in 100 aircraft being in frontline service by September. The first of 100 better armed Hawk 75A-2s had also begun to reach French fighter units by then too. A further order for 135 six-gun, Twin-Wasp engined Hawk 75A-3 was placed on 9 October, with 395 Cyclone powered Hawk 75A-4s also being acquired.

As early combat with Bf 109s during the 'Phoney War' quickly showed, the Hawk 75 was, however, no match for the latest German and British fighters. An example was flown against a Spitfire by the Royal Aircraft Establishment between 29 December 1939 and 13 January 1940, and although it was found inferior to the British fighter, the Hawk's superb manoeuvrability was favourably commented on.

Following the fall of France, the Hawk 75 entered service with the RAF by default when the outstanding French contracts were transferred to Britain. Thus, from the summer of 1940, large numbers of Hawk 75A-4s began arriving in England. Across the Channel, in the wake of the French collapse, the newly formed Vichy government retained the units equipped with Hawk 75A-1, A-2 and A-3 variants. Eventually, some 204 ex-French aircraft were taken on RAF strength, and later in the war nine ex-Iranian Hawk 75A-9s and five ex-Norwegian Hawk 75A-8s were received, plus at least one of unknown provenance.

In Britain, in accordance with RAF practice, the Hawks were appropriately named 'Mohawk' after the warlike North American Indian tribe. The mark numbers of these aircraft equated, where applicable, to the sub-series number – thus, Cyclone engined A-4s (and later A-9s) became Mk IVs. Following the fitting of British equipment, the Mohawks IVs were issued to Maintenance Units as a reserve against possible emergencies. However, by 1941 Germany had abandoned its plans to invade Britain, and other uses for the aircraft were sought. Most Mohawk IVs were eventually shipped overseas, with 90 being allocated to the Middle East and others being shipped to India.

Other Hawks had been ordered before the war by the Norwegians, although only a few had been delivered prior to the German invasion – most of these were later sold to Finland. However, when the Norwegian government established a training school at Island Airport, in Toronto, using the aircraft from existing orders (including a batch of Hawk 75A-8s), these were commandeered by the Allies. The Hawks were used for fighter training by a number of Norwegian pilots who later achieved ace status flying with the RAF.

Following the German occupation of Scandinavia in April 1940, the Royal Norwegian Air Force established a training school at Toronto, in Canada, which used previously ordered Hawk 75A-8s. A number of future Norwegian aces such as Sgt Svein Heglund received their initial fighter training on these aircraft prior to flying with the RAF (*Royal Norwegian Air Force*)

BATTLE FOR FRANCE

In the late 1930s, as international tensions mounted, many European nations seeking to rapidly improve or expand their air forces looked to the United States to make up the shortfall in the volume of aircraft being produced by their own domestic aviation industries. France led the way in terms of the number of aircraft procured when it selected both fighter and bomber types for rapid delivery to the *l'Armée de l'Air*.

As explained in the previous chapter, the French government placed a series of large orders for export variants of the Curtiss P-36A, marketed as the Hawk 75. The first examples were delivered to Reims between February and May 1939, and they subsequently re-equipped four fighter groups, namely *Groupes des Chasse* I/5, II/5, I/4 and II/4. Throughout the spring and summer of 1939, pilots trained assiduously to become familiar with their new fighter, and when war with Germany was declared on 3 September they flew France's most modern aircraft. The Hawk was a popular mount whose manoeuvrability and ruggedness would soon be tested in battle.

On 27 August 1939, further to the general mobilisation of the air force, the four *Groupes*, each equipped with 26 Hawk 75s, left the large base of Reims and deployed to smaller operational airfields closer to the border. On 3 September they were ready, but the declaration of war did not immediately lead to a land offensive. Instead, a period that became known as the 'Phoney War' commenced, where action mainly occurred in the skies. In France, most of these encounters took place along the German frontier, and GCs II/4 and II/5, both stationed in the east of the country, took advantage of their location to engage the enemy.

Following the first successes of 8 September 1939 that were detailed in the previous chapter, GC II/4, based at Saint-Dizier, continued to mount daily incursions into Germany. Towards the end of the month, Luftwaffe fighters began to respond more aggressively to these patrols, and on 24 September future ace Adj Camille Plubeau gained his first victory when he downed a Bf 109D of JGr 152.

Hawk 75A-1 N°64 of GC II/4's 4th *escadrille* was the first Curtiss fighter assigned to future ace Adj Camille Plubeau – he claimed no victories with it. The aircraft is seen here at Reims in the late spring of 1939. All the *Groupes de Chasse* equipped with the Hawk 75 were based here prior to the outbreak of war (*L Persyn*)

Three more 'aces-to-be' also achieved their first successes during this engagement, Adjs Georges Baptizet and Georges Tesseraud and Sgt Antoine de la Chapelle sharing two confirmed victories and a probable – JGr 152 lost three Bf 109Ds in total, with two more badly damaged.

The French pilots had immediately noticed a difference in the performance of the 'Dora' compared to the vastly superior 'Emil'. More examples of the latter (from I./JG 51 and II./JG 53) were engaged on 25 September, and the 4th *Escadrille* lost its flight commandant, Cne Pierre Claude, during the dogfight. Forced to take to his parachute, his body was found on the ground riddled with bullets. It took considerable diplomacy by the *Groupe's* commandant to avoid his own pilots being tempted to exact revenge on their opponents, as they were convinced Claude had been murdered whilst hanging helplessly beneath his parachute.

On 30 September, an escort mission for a Potez 63 photo-reconnaissance aircraft gave pilots from the 3rd *Escadrille* the opportunity to distinguish themselves. While diving to attack the Potez protected by GC II/4, four Bf 109Es of I./JG 53 did not sight the French escorts positioning themselves astern of the German machines. Two of the Messerschmitts were shot down by Cne Régis Guieu, commandant of the flight, and Adj Pierre Villey (the future ace's second kill).

One of the leading pilots of these early encounters was Adj Plubeau, who gained his third victory on 31 October (one of only two kills credited to the Hawk 75 in October 1939) when he downed a Henschel Hs 126 of 4.(H)/22 that was undertaking an observation sortie west of Creutzwald. This action was witnessed by Plubeau's squadron leader, who recalled;

'I see an aeroplane on the other side of the Rhine. I'm looking for Plubeau, but he has already left and is rushing towards an Hs 126. Everyone is charging. Such infernal to-ings and fro-ings lead us deeper and deeper into Germany. Plubeau is coming back to charge but the German is ardently defending himself – reversals, very tight bankings, climbings, everything, between 0 and 400 metres, when we alternately fire in all positions. And the enemy anti-aircraft artillery also engages us too. We have never seen so much bursting of every kind appearing so close to our aeroplanes. However, the Henschel is getting tired. The machine gunner is already killed. The pilot, probably shot too, lands his aeroplane as well as he can in a meadow – Plubeau lets him land there.'

Camille Plubeau increased his tally to four kills on 8 November when he downed a Dornier Do 17P of 1.(F)/22 during a reconnaissance mission south of Zweibrücken. GC II/4 saw further sporadic action in the final weeks of 1939, with the clash on 21 November being typical of these engagements. Late that afternoon six Hawk 75s bounced two Bf 109Es from *Stab* I./JG 52 over Hinterweidenthal, and both German aircraft were downed. One was credited to Adj Villey for his third kill and the other was shared by Sgt Chef Casenobe and Sgt Pierre Saillard.

However, Saillard was killed the very next day whilst escorting a reconnaissance aircraft over Phalsbourg. Both he and Plubeau were bounced by Bf 109Es from 3./JG 2, and although the latter managed to return to Xafévillers in his damaged Curtiss, Saillard baled out with grave wounds and died when he hit the ground, his parachute unopened.

Despite these occasional reversals, between September and December 1939, GC II/4 had claimed 14 confirmed victories and 10 probable kills.

Pilots from GC II/4 pose for the camera at Xaffévillers in the autumn of 1939. They are, from left to right, Adj Georges Tesseraud (seven kills), Adj Camille Plubeau (14 kills), Sous-Lt Bernard Girard (two kills), Lt Max Vinçotte (two kills), who became the *escadrille's* commanding officer after the death of Cne Pierre Claude, Adj Georges Baptizet (nine kills), Sgt Antoine de la Chapelle (seven kills), and Sgt Raymond Gabard (*G Baptizet*)

With the onset of a bitter winter, the unit was withdrawn to the south of France and had no further opportunity to increase its score before the German assault of 10 May 1040.

GC II/5 also found itself in anything but a 'Phoney War' during this period. The Toul-based unit's first brush with the enemy came on 20 September when future ace Sgt André Legrand downed a Bf 109E from 3./JG 53 west of Merzig – a second 'Emil' force-landed with battle damage following this clash.

Legrand belonged to the 3rd *Escadrille*, whose aircraft wore the Indian head emblem inherited from the American volunteers of the *Escadrille Lafayette* in World War 1. As mentioned in the previous chapter, GC II/5 paid a price for this success, losing two Hawk 75s to 1./JG 53.

With the late confirmation of the GC II/4 victories on 8 September, Legrand's victory on the 20th was in fact the first aerial kill officially ratified by the *l'Armee de l'Air* in World War 2.

Ten days later, three Hawk 75s from the *Groupe*, along with six Curtiss fighters from GC I/5 that had been temporarily relocated to Toul, became involved in a large-scale engagement with 15 Bf 109Es from I. and II./JG 53 west of Merzig whilst escorting a Potez 63 photo-reconnaissance aircraft of GR II/22. In a bitter, swirling fight, both sides suffered heavy losses. Future ace Lt Robert Huvet, commanding the 4th *Escadrille*, downed two Bf 109s in five minutes, while Sgt Chef François Lachaux got a third. Overall, JG 53 had three pilots killed and four 'Emils' shot down (and a fifth badly damaged) by the French Hawk 75s.

However, on the debit side, Sgt Jean Magnez of GC 4/5 was killed, as were two pilots from GC I/5 – the latter unit also had a third aircraft written off due to battle damage upon its return to Toul.

By this time the Allied print and film press had begun to publicise the successes being accrued by the Hawk 75 pilots, publishing a number of reports on Legrand in particular. Undoubtedly the aerial action that garnered the most media attention in these early months in the West occurred on 6 November. That day, nine Hawk 75s from GC II/5 took off to protect a Potez 63 that was conducting yet another reconnaissance mission over the Franco-German border. At 1450 hrs, two formations totalling 27 Bf 109Ds from JGr 102 attacked the French aircraft.

Determined to take advantage of their numerical superiority, the German fighters pressed home their attacks for almost 30 minutes in what became known in the French press at the time as 'the fight of the 9-versus-27'. Sgt André Legrand found himself in the thick of the action;

'I pursued a Messerschmitt that was attacking Asp Lefol. I went into a dive behind a '109, which, after dives and a series of reversals, led me to a position northeast of Metz, near Moselle, where I shot him down. Climbing up to rejoin my patrol, I met Adj Dugoujon. We climbed up to 6000 metres but saw nothing. However, as I looked off to the north, I spotted seven Me 109s heading for us – I warned Dugoujon.

'After a short hesitation, we decided to climb still higher in an effort to fight off the enemy patrol. A '109 pulled away from the formation so as to attack us from the rear. A second one also broke off, and it would attack me from head-on a little later in the action. Dugoujon dived and attacked. I waited for a few seconds. Two enemies charged behind Dugoujon and I attacked them, despite two more fighters getting in behind me from above. I then went after one of the Me 109s that had dived on me, the pilot accepting the individual fight.

'Within two turns I was on the tail of his aircraft, and I fired. He dived, and at about 1500 metres his propeller stopped – I had started shooting when we were both at a height of 6000 metres. I gave him up and went after two more assailants, but they fled. Thus ended the fight.'

With his Hawk 75 now short of fuel, Legrand was unable to return to Toul, and he was forced to land in a field near Lesse. He immediately telephoned his commanding officer to reassure him that he was okay, and to lodge his two victory claims. Legrand was in turn told the incredible news that the remaining pilots had got safely back to base, although Sgt Trémolet had had to belly-land his damaged Hawk 75.

The French fighters were credited with the destruction of five Bf 109s – one to Asp Georges Lefol and two each to future aces Sgt Edouard Salès and Legrand. There were also claims for several probables, and three Bf 109Ds did indeed return to base with varying degrees of battle damage.

Following this one-sided clash, French and British journalists quickly, but erroneously, concluded that the *l'Armée de l'Air* fighters were clearly superior to their Luftwaffe equivalents in the various stories that dominated the front pages of the national press on 7 November. But no journalist seemed to realise that the Hawk 75s' opponents on the 6th were Bf 109Ds – a version of the Messerschmitt fighter that would soon be replaced within the Luftwaffe by the vastly superior Bf 109E.

After this apparently stunning success, the next day Sgt Salès would take his tally to four kills when he downed a Do 17P from 3.(F)/22 near Bleskastel. He and Sgt Trémolet destroyed another Dornier from this unit on 21 November, and two days later GC II/5 claimed its final victory of 1939 when the *Groupe* shared in the destruction of an He 111H-2 from 2.(F)/122 with three RAF Hurricane Is from No 1 Sqn. One of those credited with a share in its demise was future ace Sgt André Bouhy.

The three pilots that enjoyed success during the famous '9-versus-27' aerial battle of 6 November 1939 relax in the *Escadrille Lafayette* mess at Toul-Croix-de-Metz. Closest to the camera is Asp Georges Lefol, who was credited with one confirmed and one probable following the engagement. In the centre is Sgt Edouard Salès, who had scored two confirmed victories, and to the right is Sgt André Legrand, who was also credited with two confirmed kills (*J Rajlich*)

Future seven-kill ace Sgt Edouard Salès of GC II/5's 3rd *escadrille* poses for a snapshot alongside his Hawk 75A-1 N°5 at Toul-Croix-de-Metz in late 1939 (*E Salès*)

The onset of violent storms and the harshest winter weather for 50 years curtailed virtually all flying on the Western Front for much of December 1939. The first action of the new year occurred on 2 January when Hawk 75s from GC II/5 clashed with a handful of fighters from 1./JG 53 on 2 January. Two Bf 109Es force-landed following the engagement. Eight days later the *Groupe* took advantage of another rare break in the weather to mount a large patrol over the frontline in support of a photo-reconnaissance mission flown by a Potez 63.

Soon after crossing the Franco-German border, the French aircraft spotted three Bf 109Es from 1./JG 2. The Hawk 75 pilots, led by Cne Gérard Portalis, immediately swept in to attack. Portalis, and future ace Sous-Lt Pierre Villacèque, claimed the shared destruction of a Bf 109, while André Legrand shot a second one down. These were the final victories credited to GC II/5 prior to it being posted to Cannes to rest in early March. Returning to Toul in mid-April, the *Groupe* would achieve just one more aerial success prior to the commencement of the *Blitzkrieg* on 10 May, but it was a highly symbolic one. On 23 April, Sous-Lt Jan Klan claimed the first victory to fall to a Czech volunteer pilot flying with the *l'Armée de l'Air* when he shot down a Bf 109E from I./JG 52.

Elsewhere on the Western Front, Hawk-equipped GC I/4 saw only limited combat due to its location in northern France. Indeed, its pilots claimed just four victories during the 'Phoney War'. One of these was a rare Do 17S-0 of 1.(F)/Ob.d.L., which, attempting to take advantage of clear skies, tried to fly a photo-reconnaissance mission over southern England on 13 January 1940.

Cne Bernard Barbier and future ace Sgt Georges Lemare intercepted the aircraft and forced it to belly land near Calais. One of only three Do 17S-0s built for high level reconnaissance, it was captured virtually intact with it a mass of photographic equipment on board. This was the first success for Lemare, who later became an ace on the Eastern Front serving with the famous *Normandie-Niemen* Regiment.

GC I/5 was only slightly more successful, claiming eight confirmed victories and two probables prior to May 1940. Based at Suippes, in Champagne, it was also too far from the border to intervene, and so the *Groupe's* pilots had only rare opportunities to pit themselves against the Luftwaffe. However, on 30 September, a six-aircraft patrol involving fighters from both GCs I/5 and II/5 (the former being detached as reinforcements to Toul) saw the *Groupe* claim its first kills. Three 'Emils' from I./JG 53 were downed (two by GC I/5) west of Merzig, although three Hawk 75s were lost and two pilots from GC I/5 killed.

The *Groupe's* next success came on 11 January when it brought down a Do 17P of 3.(F)/11 that was attempting to fly a photo-reconnaissance mission over Verdun. Future aces Lt Edmond Marin-la-Meslée

Czech volunteer pilots Sous-Lts Josef Jaske and Jan Klan served with GC II/5's 4th *escadrille* at Toul-Croix-de-Metz. They are seen here in February 1940 standing alongside Hawk 75A-2 N°145. Klan, who would claim five kills flying the Hawk 75, was the first Czech pilot to be credited with a victory in the Curtiss fighter on 23 April 1940 (*J Rajlich*)

Pilots from GC I/5's 1st *escadrille* pose with a souvenir taken from the Do 17P that the unit shot down on 11 January 1940. They are, from left to right, Sgt Gérard Muselli, Sgt Léon Vuillemain, Lt Edmond Marin-la-Meslée, Cne Jean-Mary Accart, Sous-Lt Jean-Marie Rey, Adj Michel Emprin, Sous-Lt Georges Brian and Sgt René Rubin. Most of them would become aces in May 1940 (*G Brian*)

and Sous-Lt Jean-Marie Rey claimed the victory. However, to their undoubted frustration, fellow future aces Cne Jean-Mary Accart and Sgt Gérard Muselli were only credited with a shared probable kill against a second Dornier intercepted that same day.

With the return of the sunny days in April, incursions by the Luftwaffe became increasingly numerous, and included penetrations deep into French territory. GC I/5 soon found itself in the thick of the action, and on 7 April future aces Lt Michel Dorance and Sous-Lt François Warnier each shot down a Bf 110 from I./ZG 2 south of Sedan. Adj André Salmand died in the same action, his fighter being seen to suddenly dive away. It is believed that his Hawk 75 suffered oxygen failure and he passed out.

Four days later, future aces Sous-Lt Hubert Boitelet and Sgt Maurice Tallent joined forces with three Morane MS.406 pilots from GC III/6 and GC III/7 to bring down a Do 17P from 5.(F)/122. The photo-reconnaissance aircraft came down east of Reims.

Despite these successes, it was becoming worryingly evident that the effectiveness of the Hawk 75's 7.5 mm machine guns was leaving much to be desired, especially when engaging well-armoured Dornier and Heinkel bombers. As if to prove this point, on 21 April a Do 17P from 1.(F)/123 was credited to Warnier and Tallent, although in reality the aircraft limped home to Ansbach riddled with bullet holes. The next day, the Do 17P from 3.(F)/11 that was attacked by Sous-Lt Marcel Rouquette, Adj Chef Louis Bouvard and Sgt Chef François Morel did indeed crash, the aircraft coming down near Rancimont. For future aces Rouquette and Morel, this was their first victory. It would, however, prove to be GC I/5's last before the German offensive.

With the launching of the *Blitzkrieg*, most of the Hawk 75 pilots from the *Groupe* that had enjoyed sporadic success during the 'Phoney War' would rapidly increase their scores and become aces.

THE GERMAN OFFENSIVE

At dawn on 10 May 1940, the German attack on France and the Low Countries commenced when the Luftwaffe systematically bombed key Allied airfields. The Hawk 75 *Groupes* faired fairly well in the face of this onslaught, suffering only a few aircraft damaged on the ground. The units' interception patrols that were on alert were hastily scrambled.

Led by the experienced and able Cdt Jacques-Louis Murtin, who was a leader who left nothing to chance, GC I/5 would quickly establish itself as the ranking Hawk 75 unit in the Battle of France.

The *Groupe's* first success of the *Blitzkrieg* fell to future ace Sgt Chef François Morel, who had been airborne on his own since 0445 hrs. Soon after taking off, he met some Bf 110Cs from 3./ZG 26 south of Sedan. Slipping in behind one of them, Morel fired a long burst that set an engine alight and holed a fuel tank. The pilot eventually belly-landed his aircraft near Létanne. Morel was then set upon by other Bf 110s, and although his fighter was badly shot up, he managed to limp back to Suippes and force-land.

Fellow future GC I/5 ace Sous-Lt François Warnier also belly-landed his aircraft at Suippes on 10 May.

Ten minutes after Morel had departed on his dawn patrol, long time fighter pilot Cne Jean Accart, commander of the *Groupe's* first squadron had also taken off from Suippes, accompanied by his usual wingman, Czech pilot Sgt Frantisek Perina. Accart had played a key role in shaping the tactical employment of the Hawk 75 during trials undertaken in early 1939. He had met Perina pre-war, and he greatly admired his ability as a pilot. Both men would score heavily over the next three weeks.

Heading for the frontline, they intercepted a Do 17Z of II./KG 2 that had already been badly damaged by flak during an attack on Reims-Champagne airfield. Teaming up with two Hawk 75s from GC I/4 that were also in their sector, Accart and Perina made short work of the German bomber, which belly-landed near Virginy.

Both men claimed further victories shortly after 1800 hrs when six Hawk 75s from GC I/5 intercepted Do 17Zs from III./KG 3 that had just bombed Suippes. Sous-Lt Warnier claimed two of them, one of which he shared with Sous-Lt Pierre Scotte. Sous-Lt Georges Lefol, who had participated in the famous '7-versus-27' clash whilst serving with GC II/5 in November 1939, claimed a third Dornier.

For their part, Accart and Perina had methodically shot down three of the Do 17Zs one after another.

On the opening day of the *Blitzkrieg*, GC I/5's pilots flew a total of 41 sorties, and were credited with ten victories. However, many of the *Groupe's* aircraft were damaged during the fighting, and the number of available Hawk 75s quickly decreased. Such attrition afflicted all units equipped with the Curtiss fighter, but still they fought on.

GC I/5's next big haul came at 1030 hrs on 12 May, when Hawk 75s engaged a formation of Ju 87Bs from I./StG 76 sent to attack ground targets in Sedan. Although a fearsome weapon, the German dive-bomber had suffered heavy losses when StG 2 was attacked by RAF Hurricanes on 11 May, and they again proved to be easy prey for determined fighters. The French high command granted 11 confirmed victories at the end of what was described as a 'pigeon shoot' – actual losses were three Ju 87s destroyed and two damaged.

In just 72 hours of fighting, GC I/5 had been credited with 30 confirmed victories, and six of its pilots – Accart, Perina, Marin-la-Meslée, Morel and Tallent – had already achieved ace status.

Further to the east at Xaffévillers, the Hawk 75s of GC II/4 had also been in the thick of the action since dawn on 10 May. Like GC I/5, the *Groupe* had been attacked at its base and six of its Curtiss fighters badly damaged. To have so many aircraft taken out of service at such a crucial time hit the unit hard, and it would continue to suffer from a lack of air-worthy Hawk 75s until month end.

Nevertheless, GC II/4 scrambled its remaining fighters many times over on 10 May, and lost three more aircraft (with one pilot killed and another seriously wounded) fighting He 111s and Bf 110s that same day – the *Groupe* claimed two German aircraft as confirmed victories

Sat in his Hawk 75 N°18 at Suippes, Sgt Maurice Tallent was the first pilot to become an ace in GC I/5's 2nd *escadrille*. Having claimed two victories in April, he participated in the destruction of three German aircraft on 11 and 12 May 1940. By the end of the Battle of France Tallent had increased his score to 11 destroyed and 1 probable (*E Preux*)

in return. Xaffévillers suffered a second surprise attack at 0900 hrs on 12 May, just after a patrol had returned. Approaching at low-level, Bf 109s appeared without warning and thoroughly strafed the airfield, destroying five Hawk 75s and seriously damaging three others. Several hours later, GC II/4 had Sous-Lt Gabriel Duperret shot down and killed just as he was taking off, his fighter crashing at St-Pierre-Mont.

These incidents clearly showed that Xaffévillers was well known to the enemy, so GC II/4 was told to abandon the airfield on the 14th. By then it had just 14 airworthy aircraft, many of which were not combat capable.

Toul-based GC II/5 was also committed to action soon after dawn on 10 May. Shortly after sunrise, the sound of many aero engines was heard around the airfield. Although the *Groupe's* alert patrol was ready to take-off, unit CO, Cdt Marcel Hugues (a 12-victory ace from World War 1), had been ordered by *Groupement* 22 to keep his available fighters on the ground at readiness! A subsequent attack by German aircraft lightly damaged two of the unit's Hawk 75s, and a shot-up He 111 also force-landed at Toul with its undercarriage dangling from the mountings prior to GC II/5 finally being given permission by HQ to scramble!

Throughout the Battle of France, GC II/5 rarely scrambled its alert fighters in ones and twos, as Cdt Hugues was a great believer in strength in numbers. He would order at least two patrols (totalling six aircraft) to take off at a time, and he also routinely opted for a single five-aircraft patrol, although this formation quickly proved impossible to manage in combat. The *Groupe's* results in May-June 1940 suffered as a result of Hugues' inflexibility, both in terms of the number of missions it flew and how many German aircraft it destroyed.

No such restrictions affected GC I/4 at Wez-Thuisy, on the Marne, with the *Groupe* sending its first patrol aloft at 0440 hrs on 10 May. One of its fighters was flown by future ace Sgt Jules Joire, who described the mission to his parents in a letter that he wrote that evening;

'At about 0530 hrs we saw an aeroplane (an He 111H of the 7./KG 53) some 500 metres above us, heading east. It was travelling at full speed, and while we were climbing higher, the bomber was steadily getting away from us. I closed my cowl flaps, and with my engine pulling me along more effectively than my companions, I quickly out-distanced them and managed to gain ground on my presumed enemy.

'At the moment I recognised the bomber's black crosses, a machine-gunner aboard the aircraft shot at me and severed some of my flight controls. I shot back at him with several short bursts from three-quarter rear, right and left. I quickly knocked out the aircraft's left engine, and the bomber lost altitude. Two crewmen parachuted down as the aircraft's dive became more accentuated. Seeing (Adj Jean) Hotellier and Bompain behind me, I moved away to let them finish him off. The aircraft hit the ground hard on its belly at 0600 hrs.

'Upon returning to base, I managed to carry out a normal landing in spite of the damage to my controls and my punctured tyres. I counted at least 20 bullet holes in my aeroplane, yet I was as fit as a fiddle.'

This He 111H was the first victory credited to future aces Jules Joire and Jean Hotellier.

10 May also saw GC I/4 transferred to Dunkirk, in northern France, from where it would operate over northern Belgium and the Netherlands.

Sgt Jules Joire of GC I/4's 1st *escadrille* stands in front of his Hawk 75 N°115. He was awarded the first of his six confirmed victories shortly after dawn on 10 May 1940. Joire was subsequently wounded whilst flying this aircraft on 25 May when he was hit by defensive fire from a Do 17 that he was attempting to shoot down. The ace force-landed at Loeuilly and was admitted to hospital in Beauvais, from where he was evacuated to England (*J Joire*)

The following afternoon, the *Groupe* sortied all 26 of its Hawk 75s to provide cover for Allied troops that were withdrawing into the region. At 1640 hrs, the unit clashed with Bf 109Es from III./JG 26 that were escorting He 111Ps from KG 54. The latter were reconnoitering roads near Antwerp that were being used by retreating troops.

GC I/4 claimed the destruction of three Bf 109s and two He 111s. Among the successful pilots were Cne Louis Delfino and Sgt Chef Johannès Cucumel, both of whom would join Bloch 152-equipped GC II/9 a few days later and ultimately become aces. However, GC I/4 suffered grievously in return, having two pilots killed (including *Groupe* commander Cmdt André Hertaut) and three wounded. Aside from the five Hawk 75s that were shot down, many others received damage to varying degrees. The next morning, GC I/4 could only field six flyable aircraft, and it would take several days for it to recover from this mission.

——— BREAKTHROUGH IN SEDAN ———

At dawn on 13 May, the Germans focused their attention on Sedan as phase two of the 'Dyle' manoeuvre, which would encircle Allied troops in the north and ultimately lead to the Dunkirk evacuation. With the delivery of replacement aircraft proving to be a painfully slow process for fighter units in the *l'Armée de l'Air*, and GCs I/4, II/4 and II/5 being based a considerable distance away from Sedan, only GC I/5 had sufficient Hawk 75s on strength to respond to the new offensive.

At 0700 hrs, the interception of a formation of six He 111Hs from 6./KG 55 allowed the commander of GC 2/5, future ace Lt Michel Dorance, to score his third and fourth victories – these were both shared with future ace Sous-Lt Michel Parnière. Future Czech ace Lt Tomas Vybiral also participated in Dorance's first kill, despite having only joined GC I/5 the previous day.

Later that same morning, nine Hawk 75s from GC 1/5 were on patrol over Stonne when they were bounced by Bf 109Es from II./JG 53. The French pilots were quickly overwhelmed, but not before Lt Marin-la-Meslée had shot down a Bf 109. Despite the numerical advantage enjoyed by the German fighters, only one Hawk 75 was lost. Its pilot, Lt A Vrana (one of 113 Czech airmen that flew with the *l'Armée de l'Air* during the Battle of France), successfully baled out.

During the following days, the *l'Armée de l'Air*, outnumbered as it was, was unable to ensure adequate fighter coverage over the rapidly crumbling front. This in turn gave the ever-present enemy bomber formations carte blanche to attack retreating Allied troops virtually at will. The German breakthrough was inevitable, especially with the effective support being provided by the Luftwaffe to the advancing Wehrmacht.

Enemy troops relied heavily on aerial intelligence of Allied positions during the lightning advance of the *Blitzkrieg*, and much of this information came from Hs 126 observation aircraft. Acting as the eyes of the advancing *Panzers*, the Henschel's slow speed and agility made it difficult to intercept. And more often than not, by the time a French fighter had been scrambled following a report reaching its base that an Hs 126 was active over the frontline, the Henschel had usually departed, its job done. Even when this was not the case, the German crews flying these aircraft proved eminently capable of looking after themselves in the few combats that took place between Allied fighters and Hs 126s.

For example, on 15 May it took seven aircraft from GC I/5 to shoot down a single Henschel from 1.(H)/10 southeast of Sedan. And the French pilots involved were not novices either, as aces Marin-la-Meslée, Dorance, Rey, Lefol and Vuillemain all received a share in the credit for the Hs 126's demise. Three more aces – Guieu, Baptizet and Casenobe – from GC II/4 managed to damage a second Henschel from 1.(H)/14 that same day (which the French listed as destroyed), while on the 16th five pilots from GC I/5 (including aces Dorance, Warnier, Bressieux and Tallent) and some from GC II/5 (including aces Monraisse and Legrand) brought down an Hs 126 from 1.(H)/12.

Although a number of observation aircraft were claimed by Hawk 75 pilots, far more bombers fell to the guns of the Curtiss fighter during the Battle of France. When attacking a large formation of He 111s, Do 17s or Ju 88s, the French pilots not only had to fight their way through the screen of defending fighter escorts, but also penetrate the bomber formation's wall of defensive fire. In an effort to reduce the effectiveness of the latter, Curtiss pilots would attempt to isolate their opponents by breaking up the tightly packed formations. And because of the Hawk 75's light armament, they had to get in close to their opponents so as to inflict any kind of telling damage.

Unlike RAF fighters of the time, the Hawk 75 was not fitted with an armoured windshield, so attacking pilots were exposed to considerable hazard at such close quarters.

Employing these very tactics, GC I/5 enjoyed terrific success against I. and II./KG 55 during the early afternoon of 18 May. Three patrols of Hawk 75s (nine aircraft in total) were taking it in turns to cover Fismes, in the Marne region. On the ground, the Allies were assembling troops to help reinforce the beleaguered Aisne front. At around 1530 hrs, Hawk 75s from GC I/5 intercepted a formation of 20 unescorted He 111Ps from I. and II./KG 55 that had been sent to bomb rail targets west of Fismes. Led by Cne Jean Accart, the nine Curtiss fighters managed to prevent the bombers from hitting their target, and then did their utmost to isolate them from one another. Following a hard fight, the French pilots were credited with the destruction of six Heinkels (five were actually shot down and three returned to base with battle damage).

The *Groupe* had paid a high price for its success, however. Marin-la-Meslée force-landed his damaged Hawk 75 at Suippes, as did fellow ace Gérard Muselli. The aircraft of Accart, Rouquette, Vuillemain and Vasatko also bore the scars of the battle, but two of GC I/5's most prolific pilots did not make it back. Sous-Lt Jean-Marie Rey, who had nine victories to his name, crash-

Pilots of GC I/5's 2nd *escadrille* come together for a photograph at Suippes just prior to the *Blitzkrieg* commencing on 10 May 1940. These men were responsible for making GC I/5 the most successful French Hawk 75 unit during the Battle of France. They are, from left to right, Sgt Maurice Tallent (11 kills), Sgt Chef Jérémie Bressieux (eight kills), Sous-Lt Michel Parnière (eight kills), Lt Tomas Vybiral (seven kills), Lt Michel Dorance (14 kills), Sous-Lt Georges Lefol (12 kills), Sous-Lt François Warnier (eight kills), Sous-Lt Hubert Boitelet (five kills), Sgt Jean Girou (seven kills) and Sgt André Delparte (one kill) (*J Bressieux*)

landed after being hit in the thigh by defensive fire from an He 111P. Badly wounded, he would take no further part in the Battle of France.

Sgt Chef François Morel's fighter was also hit shortly after he had claimed his ninth and tenth victories. With his Hawk 75 burning fiercely, the apparently unscathed Morel took to his parachute. As he floated down to earth he was possibly struck by groundfire from trigger-happy French infantrymen and badly wounded in the head. Following several weeks in hospital, Morel would succumb to his wounds on 17 June.

In his book *Chasseurs du Ciel,* Jean-Mary Accart (who shared in the destruction of three He 111s with Vasatko and Muselli) recounted this mission;

'If only, like the Me 109s or 110s, or the Blochs, Moranes and Dewoitines, we had cannons as well as machine guns, I am confident that with the potential represented by my nine pilots there would have been more German bombers on the ground without us having to endure the torrid crossfire of the He 111s. We could have knocked out engine oil and fuel lines from a more comfortable distance of some 200 metres, with two or three shells per engine being sufficient, rather than having to close to 50 metres before filling our targets with machine gun rounds in order to inflict any damage. The story of this mission could have been so different.'

Both GCs II/4 and II/5 were also in action on 18 May, encountering all manner of German aircraft. During its only mission of the day, the ten available Hawk 75s of GC II/4 initially intercepted an Hs 126 of 2.(H)/23 west of Rethel, which was shot down by four pilots (including aces Guieu, Rubin and Paulhan). A second Henschel escaped, however, when a number of Bf 109Es from 7./JG 53 intervened. One of the Messerschmitt pilots was quickly isolated by Sous-Lt Plubeau and shot down. His companions then broke off and fled east.

Barely five minutes later, the Hawk 75s engaged the same formation of He 111Ps from I. and II./KG 55 that had been attacked by GC I/5. Two aircraft from 4./KG 55 were downed, with aces Guieu, Rubin, Paulhan and Plubeau all sharing in these successes. A second group of bombers then appeared on the scene, but these aircraft were escorted by Bf 109Es from I./JG 76, which immediately attacked. The resulting dogfight was very confused, but the pilots of GC II/4 made the most of the superb handling of their Curtiss fighters and two 'Emils' were shot down (one of which was shared between Rubin, Paulhan and Plubeau).

The German pilots in turn damaged Guieu's Hawk 75, and he landed at Condé-Vraux. The remaining five aircraft returned to Orconte with varying degrees of battle damage. Proving that overclaiming was rife by both sides during the Battle of France, the 'Emil' pilots involved in this action were credited with having destroyed all six Hawk 75s!

GC II/5 fought the final action of the day when it ran into 8./JG 52 east of Metz at 1740 hrs. The unit had two Hawk 75s shot down and a third machine badly damaged, and was credited with a single Bf 109E destroyed in return.

Following its afternoon of action on 18 May, the next day GC II/4 could only roster six serviceable aircraft, and it would have to wait until the 24th before it could put a more substantial force into the air.

On the 25th, replacement Hawk 75s arrived for the various *Groupes.* That same day GC II/4 suffered a serious blow when Sgt François

A line up of Hawk 75s belonging to the 'Red Devils' of GC II/4's 3rd *escadrille* at Marignane in March 1940. Seen nearest to the camera is Adj Chef Antoine Casenobe's Hawk 75A-2 N°189, nicknamed *Fanfan la Tulipe*. On 18 May, *escadrille* commanding officer Cpt Régis Guieu used the aircraft to claim a share in the destruction of an Hs 126 and two He 111s (*J Prott*)

Diétrich and Adj Pierre Villey (who had five victories to his name, including one claimed on 8 September 1939) were killed when they collided over Machault whilst fighting with Bf 109Es from 1./JG 53.

BATTLING ON FROM DUNKIRK

Despite having suffered terrible losses on 11 May, within 48 hours GC I/4 was able to resume operations over Belgium and the Netherlands from its base at Dunkirk. The unit was particularly active in the Antwerp sector, with one its busiest days being 17 May. Late that afternoon, whilst patrolling over Beveland, nine Hawk 75s from GC 1/4 were bounced by Bf 109Es from I./JG 20. Two Curtiss fighters immediately burst into flames and both pilots, although wounded, took to their parachutes – a third fighter belly-landed at Mardyck. Their squadronmates enjoyed better fortune, however, and three of them would claim a Bf 109 destroyed apiece (I./JG 20 lost two 'Emils'). The successful pilots were Sgt Jules Joire, Adj Jean Hotellier and Lt Edmond Guillaume, and these three aviators would ultimately become the only Hawk 75 aces of GC I/4.

Guillaume was a 36-year-old reservist who had a particular preference for 'his' Hawk 75A-1 'N° 78'. Although the aircraft was equipped with just four machine guns, Guillaume noticed that it handled better than the later Hawk 75A-3s fitted with six machine guns.

Guillaume became GC 1/4's third commander since 10 May following this action, as its previous CO, Lt J-L Hirshauer, was wounded in the foot and forced to crash-land during the course of the engagement. The latter had in turn replaced Cne P O'Byrne, who had been wounded in the hand by return fire from a Do 17Z of II./KG 2 during the unit's very first action in response to the German offensive.

On 18-19 May, the *Groupe* continued to cover troops withdrawing in the Antwerp and Ghent sectors. However, with the Germans rapidly advancing to the west, GC I/4 faced the possibility of being cut off. The evacuation order was finally passed during the night of 19 May, and the delay in pulling the unit out seriously affected the *Groupe's* combat efficiency. Prevented from joining other *l'Armée de l'Air* fighter units at Villacoublay, near Paris, until it was almost too late, GC I/4 had been reduced in strength to just 22 pilots and 18 Hawk 75s by the time it departed Dunkirk.

Some of its groundcrew were evacuated by air, but most were captured a few days later at Dunkirk and Berck. All spare parts, support vehicles and any unserviceable fighters had to be abandoned to the enemy too.

Despite this upheaval, GC I/4 still managed to undertake several patrols from Villacoublay during the afternoon of 20 May. Considerable efforts were then made to reconstitute the unit to an effective operational level, although finding replacement Hawk 75s and ground equipment proved challenging.

The *Groupe* suffered its next combat loss on 25 May when six-victory ace Sgt Jules Joire was wounded by return fire from a Do 17Z of II./KG 76 that he was attacking near Saint-Pol. Force-landing his fighter, Joire was hospitalised in Beauvais and subsequently evacuated to Britain.

Worse was to come for GC I/4 the following morning when it lost three pilots out of five that clashed with Bf 109Es from 1./JG 21 southwest of Douai. Lt André Stiquel was killed and two were wounded, one of whom was five-victory ace Adj Hotellier – both he and Sgt Raoul Bès were captured. Three 'Emils' were shot down in return (two fell to MS.406s of GC III/1, which were also involved in this action), with Lt Guillaume being credited with two of them to take his tally to exactly five victories.

Of the 14 pilots assigned to GC 1/4 on 10 May, only three remained with the squadron at Villacoublay by the evening of the 26th.

The last week of May proved to be a relatively quiet time for the Hawk 75 *Groupes*, with the aircraft downed on the 26th being the final examples of the Curtiss fighter lost that month. This was because the Luftwaffe was focusing its attention on opposing Operation *Dynamo* – the epic evacuation of the British Expeditionary Force from Dunkirk, and surrounding areas. All of the Hawk 75 units were based far to the south of the Channel coast, as the French prepared to defend Paris.

Only Luftwaffe reconnaissance or observation aircraft were encountered during this period, thus giving the battered fighter units of the *l'Armée de l'Air* the opportunity to regroup and make good their combat losses, and prepare for further intense action in June. Despite being on the verge of total collapse, and therefore badly disorganised, the French Staff did its best to hastily strengthen and stabilise the Aisne front, which it hoped would hold the advancing Wehrmacht.

However, once freed from attacking the Dunkirk evacuation, the German war machine turned its full attention to resuming the offensive to the south. The fighter units within the *l'Armée de l'Air* would continue to engage the Luftwaffe well into June 1940, but their valiant efforts were ultimately not enough to influence the outcome of the fighting.

THE GERMANS TO THE SOUTH

The aerial activity in central France gradually escalated in early June, with GC I/5 being exclusively involved in the action on the first day of the new month. The *Groupe* completed 48 sorties and claimed three victories, although it lost one of the leading Hawk 75 aces in the process.

Heading a patrol of three Curtiss fighters, Cne Jean-Mary Accart (whose tally now stood at 12 destroyed and 4 probables) was hit in the face by several splinters when his fighter was struck by crossfire from a section of He 111Hs from 9./KG 53 that he was attacking near Frasne. Although Accart managed to bale out, he hit the fin of his aircraft and seriously injured his arm, leg and face. Hospitalised in Pontarlier, Accart survived against the odds, despite having a large steel splinter embedded in his skull between his eyes. His deputy, and future ranking Hawk 75

Adj Jean Hotellier was one of only three pilots from GC I/4 to attain ace status. His Hawk 75 N°115 wore the inscription *FRANC* just forward of the cockpit. This aircraft was lost on 25 May whilst being flown by fellow ace Sgt Jules Joire. The following day, Hotellier was forced to bale out of Hawk 75 N°109 when it burst into flames after being attacked by a Bf 109E. Suffering from terrible burns, Hotellier was taken to a hospital in Cambrai, where he was captured by German troops (*J-C Hotellier*)

ace, Lt Edmond Marin-la-Meslée, replaced him as the CO of GC 1/5.

In the early afternoon of 3 June, the Germans launched Operation *Paula*, which specifically targeted *l'Armée de l'Air* airfields around Paris, as well as communication sites and industrial complexes. The Allies had known about this offensive for some time thanks to wireless intercepts and intelligence sources. The French counter-operation was codenamed *Tapir*, and it was hoped that this would negate Luftwaffe attacks on key targets.

Once German aircraft were spotted heading for Paris in great numbers, alerting messages were immediately radioed out to *l'Armée de l'Air* fighter bases from the French communications centre located within the Eiffel Tower. However, thanks to effective German radio interference, the first warning that most fighter units received was when local AA batteries opened up and enemy bombs started detonating amongst their aircraft on the ground!

The only Hawk 75 unit in a position to get its fighters aloft was GC I/5, its CO, Cdt Murtin, leading 19 aircraft into action near Reims against 30 Do 17Zs from KGs 3 and 76. The bombers were well protected by Bf 109Es from JG 2 and Bf 110Cs from ZG 26, and they inflicted a heavy toll on the badly outnumbered Hawk 75s. The escorts did such a thorough job that only a single Dornier was damaged by GC I/5, which had three aircraft shot down and one badly damaged. One pilot was killed and one badly wounded (ace Sous-Lt Michel Parnière), with a third pilot (ace Lt Frantisek Perina) suffering superficial injuries.

The *Groupe* claimed that five German fighters had been destroyed (the Luftwaffe reported the loss of three Bf 109Es and a single Bf 110C during this action), with the successful pilots including aces Marin-la-Meslée, Vuillemain, Muselli, Bressieux and Czech volunteer Vasatko.

The latter pilot's shared victory on 3 June took his tally up to eight confirmed. Vasatko had only joined the *Groupe* on 12 May, and within six days he had already claimed five successes to make ace. He would claim a further four victories during the campaign in France, and later scored two kills while serving with the RAF. Rising to the rank of wing commander, Vasatko was killed in combat flying a Spitfire whilst leading the Exeter Wing on 23 June 1942.

Meanwhile, at Toul, GC II/5 again missed out on most of the action during the opening attacks of Operation *Paula*. Nine aircraft were scrambled at 1330 hrs, and nine more were made ready for take-off at short notice. However, at 1400 hrs, Cdt Hugues, having not received the word to send the latter machines aloft, decided to break for lunch! When orders reached Toul for more aircraft to scramble, there were no pilots on the airfield. Hugues was heavily criticised by his commanding officer following this episode.

These pilots from GC I/5's 1st *escadrille* participated in the destruction of three He 111Ps from I./KG 55 on 26 May. Posing in front of Cpt Jean-Marie Accart's Hawk 75 N°151 at Suippes, they are, from left to right Sgt Gérard Muselli, Sgt Chef Léon Vuillemain, Sgt Frantisek Perina, Lt Edmond Marin-la-Meslée, Cpt Jean-Marie Accart and Sous-Lt Marcel Rouquette (*J Mutin*)

By the time GC II/5's nine Hawk 75s had climbed to altitude, most German aircraft had already attacked their targets and were heading home. The Hawk 75 pilots gave chase, but upon seeing literally hundreds of enemy aircraft ahead of them, they wisely chose to return to base.

On 5 June, GC II/5 sent all of its available pilots and 20 Hawk 75s away from Toul for the day, as the unit was located too far from the frontlines to allow it to effectively protect the beleaguered French armies on the ground. Operating from Connantre, on the Marne, the *Groupe* took off in strength that afternoon to protect Bréguet 693s sent to attack enemy troops on the Somme. The formation was intercepted by Bf 109Es from II./JG 27, and the Hawk 75 pilots battled bravely to keep the enemy fighters from attacking the vulnerable bombers. The unit did its job well, as not a single Bréguet was lost.

The 'Emils' proved to be tough opponents, and one Hawk 75 crash-landed back at Connantre and four more were badly damaged. A single Bf 109E was destroyed, however. The German fighters were proving too fast for the Hawk 75s to catch, and the frustrated pilots took out their frustration on a much slower quarry on their way home – an Hs 126 of 3.(H)/13 discovered southwest of St Quentin. No fewer than nine pilots attacked the hapless Henschel, which eventually went down. Among the pilots credited with the kill were aces Cdt Albert Petitjean-Roget, Cne Hubert Monraisse, Lt Pierre Villacèque, Sous-Lt Marcel Hébrard and Czech pilot Sous-Lt Jan Klan.

Further to the west, GC I/4 had moved from Villacoublay to Evreux, in Normandy, on 1 June, having made good the losses it had suffered during the first 16 days of the *Blitzkrieg*. On the 5th, the unit returned to action when it sortied 15 fighters to protect Bréguet 693s that had been ordered to attack German forces to the south of Abbeville. Intercepted by 15 Bf 109Es from III./JG 3 west of Amiens, the Hawk 75 pilots managed to repel the fighters, claiming the destruction of seven 'Emils' (only two were shot down, however, with ace Lt Guillaume being credited with a shared kill). The unit had Lt Pierre Meyzonnier killed in return.

6 June would see more Hawk 75s shot down than on any other day in the Battle of France. Again, all the losses were inflicted by Bf 109Es, which were now present over the frontline in greater numbers than ever before. Sous-Lt Adj Jean Paulhan of GC II/4 was the first pilot to be brought down, the ace crash-landing near Cocherel at 0745 hrs after his patrol was bounced by ten Bf 109Es from 2./JG 76 over the bridges at Aisne. Paulhan was credited with destroying an Hs 126 of 4.(H)/12 northeast of Laon 25 minutes earlier.

At 1215 hrs, GC II/5 had two Hawk 75s destroyed and a third badly damaged by Bf 109Es from 2./JG 2 as the *Groupe* stoutly defended Martin 167F bombers from GBs II/62 and II/63. All three pilots survived, although there are unconfirmed reports that Lt Pierre Houzé was killed later that day whilst fighting alongside ground troops attempting to resist the Wehrmacht's advance near Besme. A single 'Emil' from 2./JG 2 was destroyed by GC II/5 in return.

In the final action of the day involving Hawk 75s, GC I/4 was overwhelmed by Bf 109Es from I./JG 3, 4./JG 3 and I./JG 76 west of Amiens at 2000 hrs. The *Groupe* was escorting a lone Potez 63 from GR I/36 at the time, and despite the best efforts of the Curtiss pilots, the

GC I/4's most successful Hawk 75 in terms of the number of aerial victories it claimed was this aircraft, N°78 (X877). The fighter was flown throughout the Battle of France by Lt Edmond Guillaume (seven victories). The four-gun Hawk 75A-2, with its Pratt & Whitney R-1830 SCG engine, was more manoeuvrable, but slower, than later versions of the Curtiss fighter (*J-C Hotellier*)

photo-reconnaissance aircraft was shot down. The action lasted just five minutes, and aside from the Potez, four Hawk 75s were lost and a fifth fighter force-landed near Bernay. Three pilots were killed and a fourth wounded. The German pilots erroneously claimed a total of ten Hawk 75s destroyed.

Despite suffering grievous losses, GC I/4 had put up quite a fight, as four 'Emils' from JG 3 had been downed and a similar number damaged – one of the Bf 109Es had fallen to the doomed Potez. Hawk 75 aces Lt Guillaume and Sgt Lemare were amongst those credited with kills, the former taking his tally to seven destroyed and one probable.

GC I/4 was rendered non-effective late the following morning when its base at Evreux was strafed by Bf 109Es. One Hawk 75 was destroyed, another left unserviceable and two damaged.

Several hours earlier, Cne Régis Guieu had become the third Hawk 75 ace to be killed in action during the Battle of France. Leading GC 3/4 from Orconte on an escort mission for a Potez 63 of GAO 1/589, Guieu had fallen victim to a Bf 109E (either from 5./JG 3 or 6./JG 53) southwest of Soissons at 0625 hrs. The French ace had claimed his sixth and seventh victories (both 'Emils') during the previous 48 hours.

On 8 June 15 pilots, and their aircraft, from GC I/5 were sent to Evreux for the day to make good the losses suffered by GC I/4. The *Groupe* duly flew three missions that afternoon, and at 1530 hrs GC 1/5 intercepted a formation of Ju 87Rs from II./StG 2 over Rouen. Aces Alois Vasatko and Marcel Rouquette each claimed a Stuka shot down, although they were both forced to belly-land their fighters minutes later after being set upon by escorting Bf 110Cs from 4./ZG 76.

NEW *GROUPE*

When the *Blitzkrieg* started on 10 May, very few six-gun Hawk 75A-3s had reached frontline units due to a scarcity of combat-related equipment such as radios and windscreen armour. However, from the 20th onward, the pace of delivery quickened, and by the end of the month sufficient aircraft were available to make good the losses suffered by the four Hawk 75-equipped *Groupes*.

Indeed, so many Curtiss fighters had been delivered that the French Air Staff decided to re-equip a fifth *Groupe de Chasse*. GC III/2 was the unit chosen, as it had lost most of its MS.406s in the fighting in the north of France. At the end of May, it moved south from Cambrai-Niergnies to Avord so as to be close to the Hawk 75 assembly factory of Bourges. Here, on 1 June, it took delivery of 30 brand new Hawk 75A-3s.

Following a hasty training and conversion period that lasted just five days, GC III/2 was declared operational on its new mounts on the 6th when Cdt Frédéric Geille led his unit back into action.

With little time available to 'make ace' in the Hawk 75, none of Geille's pilots would achieve five kills flying the fighter. Nonetheless, six MS.406 aces scored kills in the aircraft whilst flying with GC III/2.

The *Groupe* was quickly committed to action south of the Aisne, taking its Hawk 75s into combat on 8 June. Two fighters were lost, one falling to flak and a second being downed by defensive fire from German bombers – the pilot of the latter aircraft was killed. The unit had claimed two Hs 126s and an He 111 in return, with shares in these victories being credited to aces Lt Maurice Le Blanc and Sgt Chef Georges Elmlinger.

Le Blanc was successful yet again on 9 June when he helped destroy yet another Hs 126 (from 1.(H)/41) near Fismes. A short while later, however, a wounded Elmlinger force-landed his blazing Curtiss fighter in French-held territory after it had been shot up by Hauptmann Adolf Galland of *Stab./*JG 27 whilst escorting a Potez 63 near Chateau-Thierry. GC III/2 had also lost a fighter to return fire from a Do 17Z that morning.

Veteran Hawk 75 unit GC II/4 suffered losses on the 9th too. The *Groupe* flew two large-scale patrols during the course of the day, involving 17 fighters on the first operation and 18 on the second. The morning mission saw the Hawk 75 pilots intercept a formation of Do 17Zs from II./KG 76 northeast of Reims. Despite the presence of escorting Bf 109Es from II./JG 52 and III./JG 53, the *Groupe* pressed home its attack and six pilots shared in the destruction of a single bomber.

Above them, other Hawk 75s clashed with 'Emils', one of which was credited to Plubeau's guns while another was shot down by Casenobe and Paulhan (no losses were recorded by III./JG 53, however). Sadly, the latter pilot, after scoring his seventh personal victory, was badly wounded and forced to belly-land near Bouy. Sous-Lt Blanc was also shot down in the same action.

Several hours later, the *Groupe* again faced a formation of German bombers when it engaged Do 17Zs from II./KG 2 sent to attack Reims. This time I./JG 53 provided the fighter escort. Rushing into the fight, ranking GC II/4 ace Plubeau quickly shot down a Dornier and then teamed up with another Hawk 75 pilot to set a second one alight. Having taken his tally to 14 destroyed and 4 probables, Plubeau's luck ran out when he was bounced by a Bf 109E from 3./JG 53 and forced to bale out of his burning fighter southwest of Rethel. Having been wounded prior to taking to his parachute, Plubeau would play no further part in the Battle of France, and would only rejoin the *Groupe* later in the summer.

A newly delivered Hawk 75A-3 has its armament harmonised by armourers from GC I/5 at Suippes in late May 1940. This aircraft was the mount of ranking Czech ace Cpt Aloïs Vasatko until he was forced to crash-land it at Evreux-Fauville on 8 June after being hit by return fire from a Ju 87R that he duly shot down (*G Botquin*)

Sous-Lt Guillou had also been wounded in this action, yet he had managed to nurse his irreparably damaged Hawk 75 back to Orconte.

With the situation on the ground deteriorating day by day, it was becoming increasingly hard for the French fighters to intervene effectively against the now almost invincible Luftwaffe. The Hawk 75 units did their best, nevertheless, despite facing overwhelming odds. A handful of Hs 126s, Do 17s and Bf 109Es were claimed over coming days, with ace Cne Edouard

A rare snapshot of GC III/2's Hawk 75 N°225, seen here abandoned at Avord. This *Groupe*, issued with the American fighter in late May 1940, claimed 12 confirmed victories between 8 and 13 June, in addition to the 21 it had previously attained with the MS.406 (*L Persyn*)

Corniglion-Molinier from the GC III/2 *Groupe* staff being credited with a Henschel on 12 June. He had shared in one of the Hs 126 victories claimed by the *Groupe* on 8 June, and then been credited with a Bf 110 kill the following day.

Corniglion-Molinier added these successes to the two victories he had claimed flying MS.406s the previous month, and four others (one of them a balloon) credited to him during World War 1, to achieve acedom. The first of the latter kills had been scored on 23 October 1916!

Despite these victories, GC III/2 was forced to retreat south during the evening of 9 June as the Wehrmacht approached its airfield at Mourmelon.

Two days later, GC II/4 gained its last two successes when two Hs 126s were shot down. As usual, they were shared between a number of pilots, including several aces. These victories took Sous-Lt Georges Baptizet's tally to 9 destroyed and 4 probables, gave Adj Georges Tesseraud a total of 8 destroyed and 4 probables and Sgt Antoine de la Chapelle 7 destroyed and 1 probable.

That same afternoon, the *Groupe* made the first of several moves in the space of just a few days. The unit's final combat loss of the Battle of France came on 16 June when its CO, Cdt André Borne, was shot down and killed by Bf 109Es during an attempted solo reconnaissance of enemy armour near Chatillon-sur-Seine. Borne's Hawk 75 was also the last of its type to fall in combat in 1940.

The final large-scale losses suffered by Hawk 75 units came during the late morning of 13 June, when Auxerre-based GC III/2's 13-strong patrol

Hawk 75A-1 N°89 of GC II/4's 3rd *escadrille* was used by Adj Jean Paulhan to claim his seventh victory on 9 June 1940. Minutes later he force-landed near Bouy after his fighter was shot up by Bf 109Es from 7./JG 53. GC II/4 lost four Hawk 75s during this brief action, with Paulhan being admitted to Troyes hospital with serious wounds (*L Persyn*)

engaged a formation of Ju 87Bs from II./StG 77 as they headed for Esternay railway station. When the Curtiss pilots attempted to engage the Stukas, the dive-bombers' Bf 109E escort from 2./JG 27 in turn set upon the French fighters. A huge dogfight ensued, at the end of which GC III/2 claimed three Ju 87Bs destroyed and two probably destroyed and four Bf 109Es

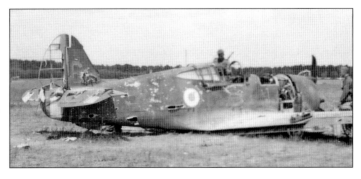

destroyed. One of each type was credited to Adj Antoine Moret, who was the *Groupe's* ranking ace with eight confirmed victories (three in Hawk 75s).

In reality, only one Stuka and one 'Emil' had been downed, although several were damaged. In return, three machines from GC III/2 were destroyed and one pilot killed and two wounded, including Cdt Geille, who was seriously burnt. The *Groupe's* sole fatality was ace Adj Maurice Romey, who had five confirmed victories with the MS.406. He had just gained his first probable kill with the Hawk 75 when he was shot down in flames by a Bf 109E. The next day, the *Groupe* retreated to pastures new.

Cpt Hubert Monraisse, commanding officer of GC II/5's 3rd *escadrille*, participated in his *Groupe's* final victory – an He 111H from 3./KG 53 – on 15 June 1940. This took his tally to six destroyed and two probables (*E Villacèque*)

GC II/5 began its retreat on 13 June, when it left its base at Toul – home since 1939. The *Groupe* obtained its last successes on 15 June when six pilots, including aces Cne Monraisse and Sous-Lts Klan and Hébrard, shared in the destruction of two He 111Hs from 3./KG 53. These successes gave both Hébrard and Klan their crucial fifth kills, and took Monraisse's tally to 7 destroyed and 2 probables.

GC I/5 abandoned Evreux for St Dizier on 12 June, and subsequently changed bases no fewer than four times in five days, so fluid was the situation on the ground. Its fighters still managed to shoot down three Hs 126s that were intercepted on the 12th, 15th and 16th to take its record to 84 confirmed victories. Of the ten pilots who shared these last three successes, no fewer than eight were aces.

On 16 June the Hawk 75 *Groupes* received orders telling them to withdraw to the French territories in North Africa. Having arrived in the south of France, GC I/4 was the first to cross the Mediterranean on 18 June. It was closely followed by GC III/2, with GC II/4 joining both *Groupes* in North Africa two days later. The final units to head south were GCs I/5 and II/5. The Battle of France had been a bitter and humiliating experience for the Hawk 75 *Groupes*, despite their best efforts to defeat the Luftwaffe.

OTHER UNITS

The pilots of the five frontline *Groupes des Chasse* were not the only ones to see action in the Hawk 75 during the campaign in France. In the days that followed the German invasion on 10 May, the *l'Armée de l'Air* HQ decided to create several small independent fighter units. They were tasked with giving fighter protection to industrial centres and strategic points, and some were equipped with Hawk 75s. A number of the flights even achieved some victories.

As previously mentioned, the factory charged with assembling the Curtiss fighter was situated at Bourges, in central France. Here, Hawk 75s were assembled following their delivery in crates by ship from the United States. Several Polish pilots were assigned to the factory protection flight, designated DAT (*Défense Aérienne du Territoire*) Bourges, on 16 May, and they claimed their first victory eight days later when Lt Wesolowski and Sgts Giermer and Kremski downed an He 111H from 8./KG 51.

The latter pilot would score again on 5 June when five Curtiss fighters scrambled and intercepted a formation of He 111s from III./KG 55. Jan Kremski, who shared in the destruction of a Heinkel with Cne Bronislav Kosinski, had claimed 1 and 1 shared kills flying a PZL PXIc in Poland on 1 September 1939. He would 'make ace' in July 1941 flying a Spitfire II with the RAF's No 308 Sqn, but was lost over France when attacked by Bf 109s the following month.

Lt Col Marcel Haegelen also shared in the destruction of another He 111 on 5 June. Like Cne Edouard Corniglion-Molinier from GC III/2, Haegelen was also a World War 1 ace. The Heinkel was his sole claim in the Hawk 75, and it took his overall tally to 23 victories (including 12 balloons), with two more probably destroyed.

On 21 June the Polish pilots of DAT Bourges joined the other Hawk 75 units in North Africa. Most of the Poles subsequently joined the RAF.

Another famous Polish pilot who flew the Hawk 75 during the campaign in France was Jan Zumbach. Assigned to MS.406 unit GC II/52, which was tasked with protecting Etampes (the unit was also known as DAT Etampes, and eventually GCD I/55), he claimed a share in a Bf 109E kill on 10 June, but was shot down minutes later. Recovering Hawk 75 N°107 from Villacoublay the following day, Zumbach flew 11 sorties in this aircraft until 17 June. He did not make any claims with the Curtiss fighter during this time, but was soon to make up for it following his transfer to the RAF. Zumbach survived the war with 12 and 2 shared victories to his credit.

Between 3 September 1939 and 25 June 1940, when the Franco-German Armistice came into effect, pilots flying Hawk 75s had claimed a total of 234 confirmed victories against the Luftwaffe. Under the *l'Armée de l'Air* system of crediting, each shared victory was given in an individual pilot's record of achievement as a full kill, not a fraction. By this method, no fewer than 38 pilots had been credited with at least five victories in the Curtiss fighter during this period.

As these statistics prove, the elegant Hawk 75 was without a doubt the mount of the aces, despite the *l'Armée de l'Air* having suffered a crushing defeat at the hands of the Luftwaffe.

A line up of Hawk 75s from DAT Bourges in late May 1940. Nearest the camera is Lt Col Marcel Haegelen's Hawk 75A-2 N°183. A World War 1 ace with 22 victories to his name, Haegelen was credited with destroying an He 111 for his 23rd kill on 5 June 1940 whilst flying a Hawk 75 (*S Joanne*)

IN AFRICAN SKIES

When the 25 June 1940 ceasefire between Germany, Italy and France came into effect, all flights by French aircraft were immediately forbidden. Thus, the *l'Armée de l'Air* was forced to remain on the ground, although by then 186 Hawk 75s that had survived the conflict had been evacuated to French North Africa – 20 more remained in southern France. However, with the signing of the Armistice, all hope of continuing the fight from across the Mediterranean vanished.

Despite the large number of aircraft still available, those units that had evacuated were in a state of some disarray, and it took time to re-organise them. Furthermore, many of the pilots that had fled to North Africa were both physically and mentally exhausted following six weeks of hard fighting, so a continuation of hostilities could not have been realistically contemplated in any case.

In the days following the Armistice, news from France was scarce, and many of the evacuated airmen could get little information about the well being of their families, or even the current status of the *l'Armée de l'Air*.

A number of fighter pilots chose to flee to Gibraltar in order to get to Britain so as to continue the fight, although none of them took any Hawk 75s. The commanding officers of the various fighter *Groupes* worked hard to maintain cohesion and discipline in their units. Nevertheless, at St Denis du Sig, near the Algerian city of Oran, Cdt Murtin of GC I/5 and Cdt Hugues of GC II/5 did consider leading their *Groupes* en masse to nearby British-held territory.

The possibility of these moves was not, of course, recorded in official archives, but many accounts from pilots in both *Groupes* at this time confirm that these officers did indeed contact the British in Gibraltar during the first week of July. They wanted to negotiate the transfer of their units and their aircraft to the RAF, but to remain under French command so as to avoid their pilots being posted to various British squadrons. Negotiations had just begun to bring both *Groupes* into the

Both GCs I/5 and II/5 based their Hawk 75s at St Denis du Sig, in French-controlled Algeria, following their escape from mainland France in late June 1940. They would commence operations from this base in early July, seeing combat against the Fleet Air Arm over Mers-El-Kébir. These particular aircraft were assigned to GC II/5 (*G Botquin*)

British fold when the tragedy of Mers-El-Kébir occurred, and Anglo-French relations plummeted.

───── FIGHTING THE FLEET AIR ARM ─────

Following the ratification of the Armistice by the French government, the status of the *Marine Nationale*, and its powerful fleet of modern capital ships, was a cause of great concern to the British government. There was a real worry that the vessels would fall into the hands of the Germans, and thus increase the threat to Britain's maritime supply routes.

Many French vessels lay at anchor in the naval base at Mers-el-Kébir, near Oran, under the command of Adm Marcel Gensoul. At dawn on 3 July, Gensoul received an ultimatum from the British. Either he rallied his ships to the Royal Navy, or he could sail and disarm them in the French West Indies or in another neutral country. However, should he refuse, the Royal Navy's Force 'H', which included the aircraft carrier HMS *Ark Royal* and the battleships *Resolution* and *Valiant*, stood by to intervene. Following an outright refusal from the French admiral, the British attacked the vessels in the harbour in the late afternoon.

At St Denis du Sig, Cdts Murtin and Hugues were availed of the worsening situation near noon. They had ignored the order issued to them several days earlier to disconnect the controls of their aircraft, thus rendering them unserviceable. This meant that the Hawk 75s of both GCs I/5 and II/5 could be operational just as soon as they were armed and fuelled. By 1400 hrs, sufficient aircraft were ready to perform a patrol overhead Oran, although the order to take-off did not come until 1800 hrs when nine Hawk 75s from GC 4/5 left St Denis du Sig. The pilots had orders to threaten and harass any intruding aircraft, but to open fire only as a last resort.

The sky over Mers-el-Kébir harbour was devoid of aircraft, but a little way out over the Mediterranean, the fighters came across a formation of 12 Blackburn Skua fighter/dive-bombers from *Ark Royal*. They watched each other for a while, and after a brief exchange of fire they separated.

More fighters took off soon afterwards as additional covering patrols were flown over the harbour, and some of the Hawk 75s from GC 3/5 intercepted Fairey Swordfish torpedo-bombers heading for the French battleship *Strasbourg*. The pilots manoeuvred in an attempt to drive them back, but the Skua escorts of 803 Naval Air Squadron (NAS) intervened. Sous-Lt Trémolet's Hawk 75 was damaged by future ace Lt J M Bruen and his observer Lt R M Smeeton. They were in turn driven off by ace Sgt Chef Legrand, who then downed Skua L2915/A7C. The latter machine's pilot, Plt Off T F Riddler, and observer, N1 Chatterley, were both killed.

However, on his return to base Legrand (whose tally now stood at nine destroyed) realised that his Hawk 75 had also been hit, and he had been saved from death by his dorsal armour plate.

Although this was to be the only air combat of the day, the French pilots felt that they could not accept what had happened in the harbour at Oran that evening, when 1300 sailors were killed by the Force 'H' attack.

GCs I/5 and II/5 remained on alert for the next few days, and GC 4/5 tangled with Skuas once again on the 6th. The French unit was credited with another confirmed victory, although all Fleet Air Arm aircraft returned to *Ark Royal* on this occasion.

The British attack on Mers-El-Kébir scuppered any prospect of the fighter *Groupes* rallying to the British cause against the Germans. Indeed, the attack convinced the Armistice commission of the usefulness in maintaining air cover in the French colonies, which were now loyal to the Vichy government. The latter, headed by Marshal Philippe Pétain, controlled Vichy France which bordered German-occupied France – the 'border' between the two ran roughly from Bordeaux to Geneva.

On Bastille Day (14 July), GC I/4 was sent to Dakar, in Senegal, on the west coast of Africa, which had also been threatened by the Royal Navy earlier that month because the modern French battleship *Richelieu* was seeking refuge in its harbour. The *Groupe* was based at Ouakam airfield, just inland from the harbour.

During August 1940, plans for the organisation of the Air Force of Vichy were issued. It would include three *Groupes de Chasse* equipped with Hawk 75s, two of which were in Morocco – GC I/5 at Rabat and GC II/5 at Casablanca, with GC I/4 remaining at Dakar. At month end, GCs II/4 and III/2 were disbanded and the remaining Hawk 75 *Groupes* equipped with 26 aircraft apiece. Following these drastic cuts in the fighter force, a large number of Hawk 75A-1s and A-2s were stored as attrition replacements. Some remained unused for more than two years.

The conditions imposed by the Armistice commission (following strict German guidelines) authorised only a one-hour maintenance flight per aircraft per week other than an operational scramble or test flights. These restrictions greatly reduced the *Groupes'* effectiveness.

Casablanca-based GC II/5 was the next unit to see action in North Africa when, on the afternoon of 14 September, Capt Hubert Monraisse (commandant of GC 3/5) led a patrol that intercepted a Saro London of No 202 Sqn off the Moroccan coast. Having first made sure that the biplane could not escape out to sea, he then opened fire. Monraisse had to throttle his fighter right back so as not to overshoot the London, and this in turn meant that his Hawk 75 was badly buffeted by the gusty conditions that blighted the area that day. His aim was good, however, and the unfortunate seaplane soon hit the water, giving Monraisse his seventh confirmed victory.

Following the Allied landings in North Africa in November 1942, Monraisse, like most former Vichy pilots, fought for the Allied cause. He was killed in action whilst strafing a train in October 1944.

At dawn on 23 September a new naval force that included Free French vessels under British command arrived off the coast of Senegal and

Hawk 75s of GC I/5's 1st *escadrille* formate for the camera during a training flight in the late summer of 1940. Following the events at Mers-El-Kébir, GC I/5 was one of the three groups equipped with the Curtiss fighter to serve with the Vichy-French *l'Armée de l'Air*. The fighter nearest to the camera is the famous Hawk 75 N°217 of Lt Edmond Marin-la-Meslée, who was the leading ace of the Battle of France with 16 victories (*J-L Claessens*)

launched Operation *Menace*. At 0600 hrs, emissaries sent by Gen Charles de Gaulle landed at Ouakam in order to rally the commander of GC I/4 to their cause. One of the emissaries was Sgt Jules Joire, a six-kill ace from the *Groupe* who had been wounded on 25 May.

Once ashore, they were met by the CO of GC I/4, Cdt de la Horie, but not before he had ordered two of his fighters into the air to fly a standing patrol over the Allied vessels, such was the level of distrust after the sad events at Oran. De la Horie was subsequently detained, although he was eventually freed by two of his officers and the emissaries in turn imprisoned. An attempt to rally other elements to the Allied cause in Ouakam proved to be unsuccessful, so the first phase of the operation had failed.

Later that same morning (23rd), Hawk 75s of GC I/4 intercepted several Swordfish from HMS *Ark Royal*. Although none of the torpedo-bombers were shot down, a Curtiss fighter was lost when it hit the water after a brief fight at low level.

At dawn on the 24th, GC I/4 maintained a permanent patrol to cover the harbour, as an attack was thought to be imminent. This did indeed prove to be the case, for at 0915 hrs three Hawk 75s intercepted six Swordfish of 810 NAS. The French fighters immediately engaged the fully armed biplanes, and the formation was dispersed. Adj Chef Abel Baillet shot down two Swordfish over the sea and future ace Sgt Georges Lemare claimed a third, as his combat report recounts;

'I attacked the last bomber from the rear, opening fire at a distance of about 50 metres. After seven or eight bursts, the English aeroplane started to turn, so I attacked a second machine from the rear. This aircraft also turned very sharply, so I broke off in search of another bomber. I quickly spotted a Swordfish heading west near the surface of the water. Diving at an angle of 60 degrees, I opened fire from 300 metres. The English aircraft made an almost circular turn and then struck the sea.'

This brought Lemare his fourth, and last, victory with the Hawk 75, and he would claim nine more kills flying Yak-9s with GC III *'Normandie-Niémen'* on the Eastern Front in 1944-45.

At 0930 hrs, the guns of the Allied naval vessels started to thunder, and Cdt de la Horie took off to spot the return fire from *Richelieu*. During this sortie he intercepted, and fired on, two aircraft that duly fled *(text continues on page 42)*.

United at Rabat, in Morocco, in October 1940 after the disbandment of GC II/4, pilots from GC I/5's 1st *escadrille* welcome Lt Camille Plubeau back following his recovery from wounds he suffered on 9 June 1940. These pilots are, from left to right, Sgt Chef Gérard Muselli (six victories), Sous-Lt Marcel Rouquette (eight victories), Adj Chef Louis Bouvard (two victories), Sous-Lt Camille Plubeau (14 victories), Lt Edmond Marin-la-Meslée (16 victories), Sous-Lt Auguste Goupy (one victory), Sous-Lt Georges Brian (one victory) and Sgt Chef Léon Vuillemain (nine victories) (*A de la Fléchère*)

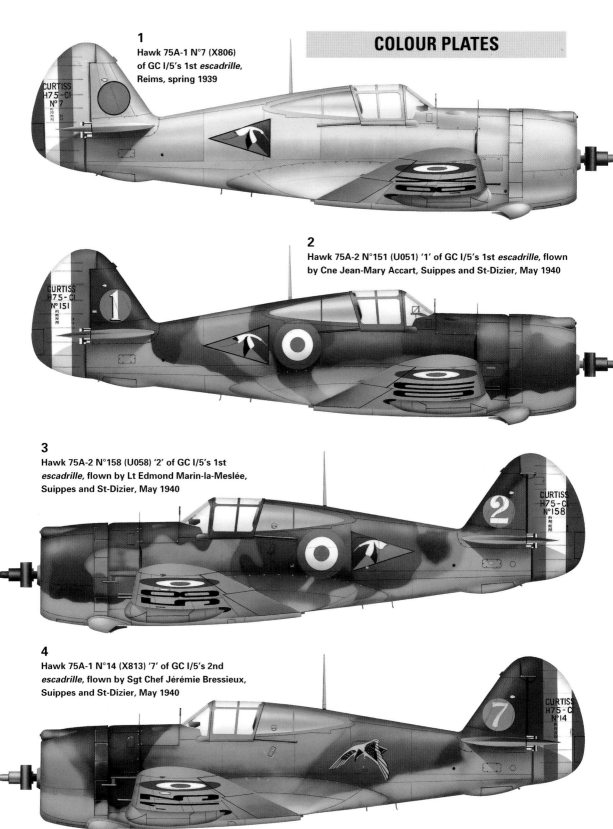

1
Hawk 75A-1 N°7 (X806)
of GC I/5's 1st *escadrille*,
Reims, spring 1939

2
Hawk 75A-2 N°151 (U051) '1' of GC I/5's 1st *escadrille*, flown
by Cne Jean-Mary Accart, Suippes and St-Dizier, May 1940

3
Hawk 75A-2 N°158 (U058) '2' of GC I/5's 1st
escadrille, flown by Lt Edmond Marin-la-Meslée,
Suippes and St-Dizier, May 1940

4
Hawk 75A-1 N°14 (X813) '7' of GC I/5's 2nd
escadrille, flown by Sgt Chef Jérémie Bressieux,
Suippes and St-Dizier, May 1940

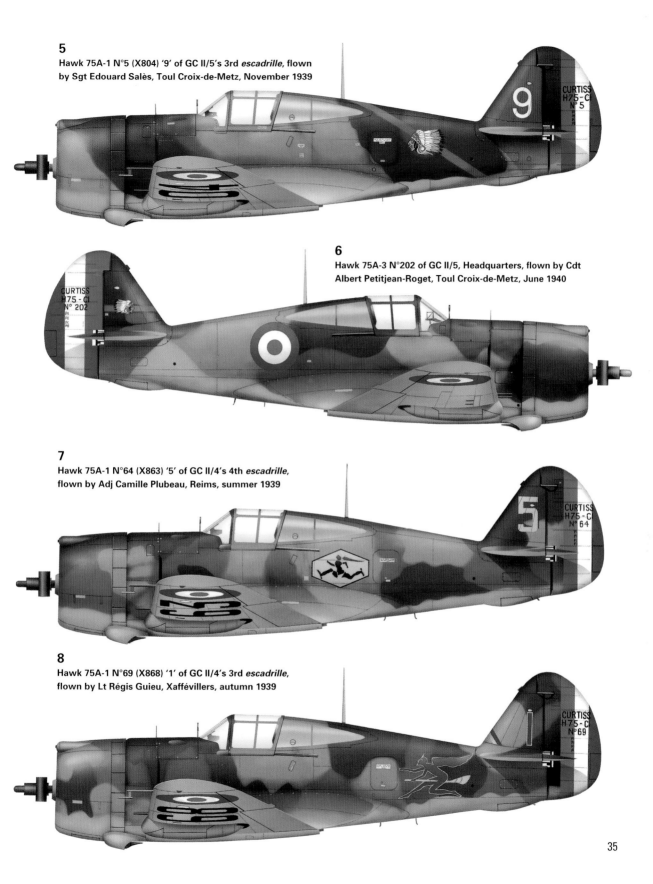

5
Hawk 75A-1 N°5 (X804) '9' of GC II/5's 3rd *escadrille*, flown
by Sgt Edouard Salès, Toul Croix-de-Metz, November 1939

6
Hawk 75A-3 N°202 of GC II/5, Headquarters, flown by Cdt
Albert Petitjean-Roget, Toul Croix-de-Metz, June 1940

7
Hawk 75A-1 N°64 (X863) '5' of GC II/4's 4th *escadrille*,
flown by Adj Camille Plubeau, Reims, summer 1939

8
Hawk 75A-1 N°69 (X868) '1' of GC II/4's 3rd *escadrille*,
flown by Lt Régis Guieu, Xaffévillers, autumn 1939

35

9
Hawk 75A-2 N°189 (U089) '7' of GC II/4's 3rd *escadrille*,
flown by Sgt Chef Antoine Casenobe, Xaffévillers and
Orconte, May 1940

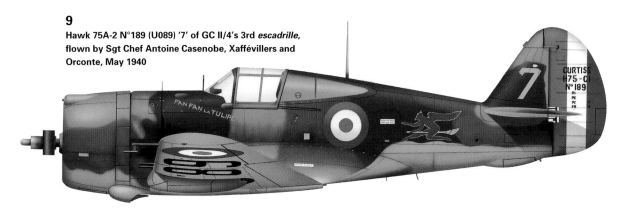

10
Hawk 75A-2 N°115 (U015) '13' of GC I/4's 1st *escadrille*,
flown by Sgt Jules Joire, Dunkerque (Nord) and
Villacoublay, May 1940

11
Hawk 75A-4 N°8 '10' of GC II/5's 3rd *escadrille*, Casablanca,
Morocco, July 1940

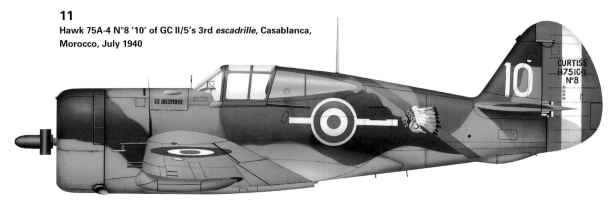

12
Hawk 75A-3 N°259 '4' of GC I/5's 2nd *escadrille*, flown
by Sous-Lt Georges Baptizet, Rabat, Morocco, late 1940

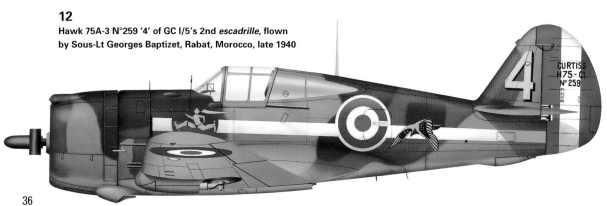

13
Hawk 75A-2 N°173 (U073) '1' of GC II/5's 3rd *escadrille*,
flown by Cne Hubert Monraisse, Casablanca, Morocco,
September 1940

14
Hawk 75A-3 N°319 '1' of GC I/4's 2nd *escadrille*, flown
by Cne Louis Delfino, Dakar, Senegal, August 1942

15
Hawk 75A-6 CUw-553/'White 3' of 1/LLv 32, flown by
2Lt Sakari Alapuro, Lappeenranta, September 1941

16
Hawk 75A-3 CUw-563/'Yellow 3' of 2/LLv 32, flown by
Capt Kullervo Lahtela, Lappeenranta, September 1941

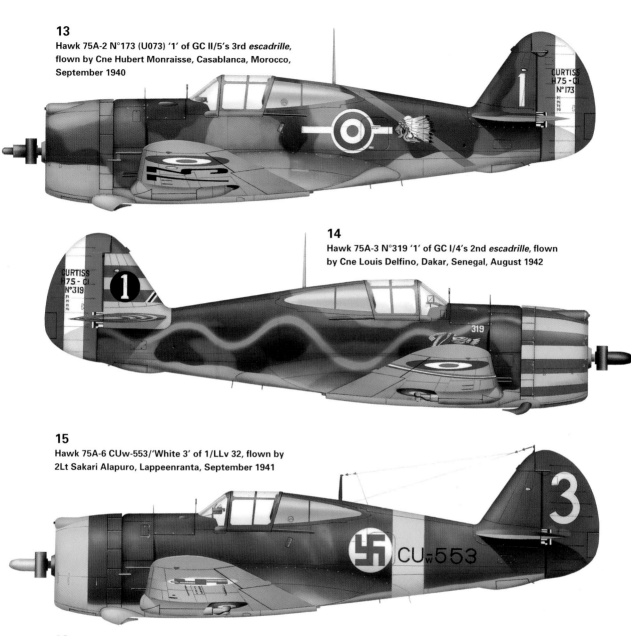

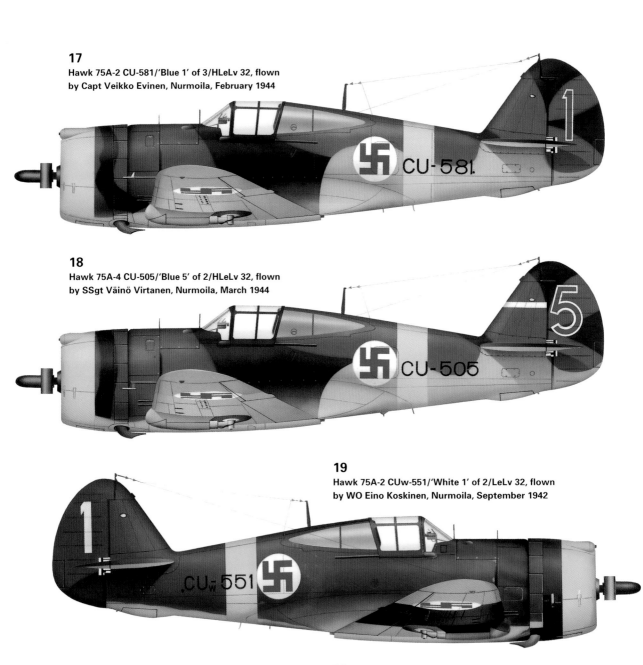

17
Hawk 75A-2 CU-581/'Blue 1' of 3/HLeLv 32, flown
by Capt Veikko Evinen, Nurmoila, February 1944

18
Hawk 75A-4 CU-505/'Blue 5' of 2/HLeLv 32, flown
by SSgt Väinö Virtanen, Nurmoila, March 1944

19
Hawk 75A-2 CUw-551/'White 1' of 2/LeLv 32, flown
by WO Eino Koskinen, Nurmoila, September 1942

20
Hawk 75A-6 CUw-558/'White 8' of 1/LeLv 32, flown
by Sgt Niilo Erkinheimo, Nurmoila, August 1942

21
Hawk 75A-3 CU-571/'Blue 1' of 3/LLv 32, flown
by Capt Pentti Nurminen, Suulajärvi, March 1942

22
Hawk 75A-2 CU-580/'Yellow 0' of 1/HLeLv 32, flown
by 1Lt Jaakko Hillo, Nurmoila, October 1943

23
Mohawk IV 2511 of No 4 Sqn SAAF, flown by
Lt H E N Wildsmith, Nakuru, Kenya, June 1941

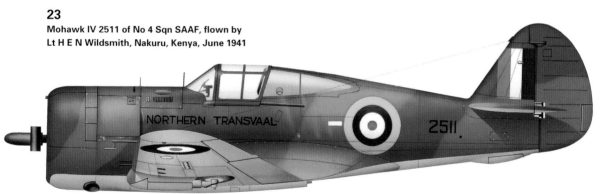

24
Mohawk IV 2514 of No 3 Sqn SAAF, flown by Capt J E Parsonson,
Aisca, Ethiopia, September 1941

25
P-36A 38-92 of the 47th PS/15th PG, flown by 2Lt Harry W Brown, Haleiwa Field,
Hawaii, 7 December 1941

26
Mohawk IV BJ546/OQ-O of No 5 Sqn, flown by Sgt C V Bargh, Akyab, Burma,
16-20 March 1942

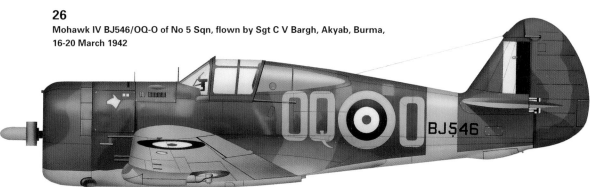

27
Mohawk IV BS788/NA-A of No 146 Sqn, flown by Sqn Ldr M B Czernin, Dinjan, Assam,
India, 23 April 1942

28
Mohawk IV 2529 of No 6 Sqn SAAF, flown by Maj M S Osler, Groutville, South Africa,
29 August 1942

29
Mohawk IV BJ442/Y of No 155 Sqn, flown by Sqn Ldr D W A Stones, Alipore, India,
30 October 1942

30
Mohawk IV BS790/WPB of No 169 Wing, flown by Sqn Ldr W Pitt-Brown, Agartala, India,
November-December 1942

31
Mohawk IV BJ439/V of No 5 Sqn, flown by Flg Off W J N Lee, Agartala, India,
February-May 1943

32
Mohawk IV BJ545/C of No 155 Sqn, flown by Sqn Ldr C G St D Jeffries, Imphal, India,
November 1943

The ferocity of the French fighters effectively disrupted further bombing attacks by Fleet Air Arm aircraft, and on the 25th another Swordfish was credited to three pilots from GC I/4, although again the aircraft returned safely to *Ark Royal*. However, a Walrus seaplane from the cruiser HMAS *Australia* was shot down by Cdt Fanneau de la Horie, and during late morning the British fleet withdrew.

Following this flurry of action, a second fighter unit was formed in Senegal in November when the autonomous 6th *Escadrille* was established at Thiès. It also received Hawk 75s, which the unit subsequently flew for almost a year.

—————— SKIRMISHES OFF AFRICA ——————

Being based in North Africa rather than the Middle East, the Hawk 75 units were spared further combat against the Allies following the invasion of Vichy French Syria and Lebanon in mid-1941. Instead, the *Groupes* concentrated on their training missions, routine test flights (there were many of these!) and formal alerts – there were not too many of the latter.

Indeed, the first action seen by the North African Hawk 75 units since Operation *Menace* took place on 29 September 1941, when Sgt Chef Georges Lemare of GC I/4 intercepted Sunderland I N9044/KG-C of No 204 Sqn off Dakar. His fire hit the big flying boat's wings, and it limped off with one of its engines damaged. However, the Sunderland's formidable defensive fire had also hit, and damaged, Lemare's Hawk 75.

Another encounter took place off Casablanca on 8 May 1942 when an unidentified aircraft was seen. Two pilots of GC II/5 quickly took off and intercepted a lone Fairey Fulmar I, and despite them claiming it destroyed upon their return to base, the British aircraft managed to make it back to its carrier.

RAF Wellingtons also occasionally tested the resolve of the Hawk 75 pilots, as the bombers would regularly undertake ferry flights from the UK to Gambia, prior to heading to units in the Middle East and North Africa. Often, the bombers would pass close to Dakar as they headed south, and GC I/4 would routinely scramble fighters to chase after them. Just such a mission was flown on 12 August 1942 by ace Capt Louis Delfino. Leading a patrol aloft in stormy weather, he still managed to intercept a Wellington. All three French pilots engaged the unfortunate bomber, which eventually crashed into the sea.

Delfino had already gained one confirmed victory with GC I/4 to add to the six he had scored flying Bloch MB.152s with GC II/9 during the campaign in France. By war's end his tally stood at 16 victories, and he returned to France as CO of GC III *'Normandie-Niémen'* in June 1945.

On 13 August another Wellington was intercepted and shot down by two pilots from GC I/4. Fifteen days later it was the turn of GC I/5 to taste success during an interception, when four Curtiss fighters were scrambled after an unidentified aircraft had been detected off the Moroccan coast. They too found a Wellington. With the restrictions on firing on Allied aircraft now far more relaxed than they had been in the summer of 1940, the GC I/5 pilots opened fire without warning. Again, the solitary Wellington had little chance of survival, and it was shot down.

Two of the victors, Lt Marcel Rouquette and Adj Léon Vuillemain, had previously distinguished themselves against the Luftwaffe, with eight

Hawk 75A-3 N°295 of GC I/4's 2nd *escadrille* was photographed on the wing in December 1941. It was assigned to future 12-victory ace Sgt Georges Lemare for two years, and he used it to claim a Swordfish destroyed on 24 September 1940. He also damaged a Sunderland whilst flying the aircraft on 29 September 1941 (*G Botquin*)

Aces Lts Pierre Villacèque and André Legrand, who served with GC II/5's 3rd *escadrille*, confronted Wildcats of VF-41 on 8 November 1942 and claimed a victory apiece over the US Navy fighters. These successes took Villacèque's score to six and Legrand's to nine. The kills came at a price, however, for both pilots had to crash-land their Hawk 75s just minutes later as GC II/5 was decimated by additional Wildcats (*E Villacèque*)

and nine confirmed victories to their credit, respectively. Both of them would later return to fight with the Allies against the Germans.

On 2 September, a patrol from GC 4/5 met three British aircraft over the coast near Casablanca. The first two managed to escape, but the third machine – a Wellington from No 69 Sqn – was forced to belly-land on a Moroccan beach. This kill gave Capt Robert Huvet his sixth victory and Sgt Chef André Bouhy his fifth. Ironically, the latter had claimed his first success on 23 November 1939 when he shared in the destruction of an He 111H of 2.(F)/122 with two RAF Hurricane Is from No 1 Sqn.

OPERATION *TORCH*

The Anglo-American landings in French North Africa, codenamed Operation *Torch*, were launched along the Moroccan coast shortly before dawn on Sunday, 8 November 1942.

At Casablanca, the pilots of GC II/5 were woken by the sounds of the bombardment from US naval vessels offshore. Rushing to the airfield at Camp Cazes, they were immediately ordered to take off, having learned that the Vichy Navy was already suffering losses. Six Hawk 75s arrived over the harbour shortly before 0600 hrs and drove off three US Navy SO2C Kingfishers that were spotting gunfire for the battleship USS *Massachusetts*. Sgt Lavie attacked the aircraft flown by Lt 'Tommy' Dougherty, who in turn force-landed in the sea before managing to beach the seaplane – he and his observer, Lt Clyde Etheridge, were captured.

Forty-five minutes later, six more Hawk 75s, led by Cdt Georges Tricaud, were in the process of taking off from Camp Cazes when 18 F4F-4 Wildcats from VF-41 (embarked in USS *Ranger*) attacked the Vichy fighters' airfield near Casablanca. Tricaud and ace Cne Robert Huvet were seen to shoot down two Wildcats between them before the former's Hawk 75 was set on fire and blew up over the airfield. Tricaud had thus, briefly, enjoyed ace status, as he had previously claimed three confirmed victories flying the MS.406 in 1940.

Moments later, Huvet, having claimed his seventh and eighth victories, and Lt de Montgolfier were also killed by the marauding Wildcats. The remaining two Hawk 75s then joined the fight, as six more from GC 3/5 took off. However, the French pilots would pay a heavy price, with aces Lts Legrand and Villacèque claiming one victory each prior to being forced to crash-land, the latter having been wounded.

During this brief, but bloody, fight, GC II/5's pilots had claimed seven American aircraft shot down. Some of these were possibly SBD Dauntlesses that were in the vicinity. Of the 18 Hawk 75s that had taken off that morning, 11 failed to return. During the course of the day, the *Groupe* had had six pilots (including two aces) killed and five wounded – GC II/5 had suffered just two air combat fatalities during the Battle of France. Few of its aircraft remained available by dusk on 8 November.

Further north at Rabat, GC I/5's CO, ace Cdt Monraisse, was absent when the alarm was raised at dawn on the 8th. Ranking Hawk 75 ace Cne Marin-la-Meslée, who commanded GC 1/5, took off without orders minutes before Wildcats from VGF-26 (embarked in USS *Sangamon*) arrived and began strafing, destroying at two Hawk 75s and other aircraft. GC I/5 flew four missions during the day without meeting any Allied aircraft. However, the situation would be very different the next day.

At 0730 hrs on the morning of the 9th, 16 Hawk 75s from the unit undertook an escort mission for LeO 451, DB 7 and Martin 167F bombers that were sent to attack Allied landing barges in the mouth of the Oued-Nefifik wadi. Little was accomplished by the bombers, and as they returned to base, eight Wildcats from VF-9 bounced the Hawk 75s out of cloud cover. Five French fighters were shot down and two pilots killed, including five-victory ace Lt Maurice Le Blanc (formerly of GC III/2, he had claimed two shared victories in the Hawk 75 in June 1940 to add to his three kills in the MS.406). Fellow ace Adj Chef Tesseraud was also badly wounded, and Lt Plubeau force-landed without injury. Adj Jérémie Bressieux was the only French pilot to emerge with a victory (his ninth, and last, success in the Hawk 75) from this one-sided dogfight.

Several hours later, five GC I/5 pilots led by Cne Marin-la-Meslée took off in the only available Hawk 75s and strafed landing vessels near Bouznika. That afternoon, five pilots from GC II/5 landed at the satellite ground of Médouina after flying in attrition replacements from Meknes. Minutes later, 13 Wildcats from VF-9 arrived overhead and strafed the airfield. All five Hawk 75s were destroyed, as were six Dewoitine D.520s and six DB 7s. GC II/5 had been so badly hit over the past 48 hours that it was now barely viable as a fighting unit, and the *Groupe* would play no further part in the action.

Two Hawk 75s from GC I/5's 2nd *escadrille* perform a patrol during 1942. N°88, furthest from the camera, was attacked by Wildcats on 9 November 1942, its pilot, ace Lt Camille Plubeau, being forced to crash-land. He emerged unscathed from the incident, despite an American bullet having exploded an oxygen bottle positioned directly behind his seat. N°88 was just one of five Hawk 75s downed by VF-9 during this one-sided engagement (*A de la Fléchère*)

Early in the evening of 11 November, the COs of GCs I/5 and II/5 received a message notifying them of the end of hostilities. Some 13 Hawk 75s had been shot down, 11 destroyed on the ground, one lost in an accident and five damaged during the first 48 hours of *Torch*. Four aces had been killed and two more badly wounded.

Following this brief, but bloody, struggle in North Africa, French West Africa quickly chose to side with the Allied cause.

In a little over two years of flying in Vichy colours, Hawk 75 pilots had gained 22 confirmed victories. Very soon, most of them would resume the fight against the common foe occupying their homeland – the Germans. Training flights resumed without any restrictions, and at the end of November 1942, GC II/5 was equipped with the Hawk 75's lineal successor, the P-40. With these aircraft, it returned to action in Tunisia in early 1943. However, GCs I/4 and I/5 would retain their Hawk 75s until the early summer, when both *Groupes* received more modern equipment.

Although it was now superseded in frontline service, the Hawk 75 still had a role to play with the *l'Armée de l'Air*. Thanks to the substantial number of aircraft that had been kept in storage in North Africa, there were plenty of perfectly serviceable examples available for use by fighter training schools in Morocco. The Hawk 75 proved to be such a good training platform that they were retained in North Africa until 1946, when the survivors were flown back to France to operate from Cazaux. The last Curtiss fighters would linger on until the summer of 1949.

EAST AFRICAN DEBUT

By mid 1941, the South African Air Force (SAAF) had been fighting against the Italians in Ethiopia and Somaliland for a year, and although all but defeated in the latter country, enemy forces continued to stubbornly resist in central Ethiopia. The SAAF was in desperate need of more modern equipment, and with the campaign in North Africa taking priority, the Mohawk provided a suitable, if not ideal, solution.

During the spring of 1941 the first of 86 aircraft to enter SAAF service were delivered to Eastleigh, near the Kenyan capital of Nairobi. On 2 May, No 4 Sqn formed at Nakuru, in Kenya, under the command of Maj A C Barratt. Among its number was future desert ace Lt Andrew Bosman, and Lt Hugh Wildsmith who ended the war with four kills. By June the squadron had received 14 Mohawk IVs at

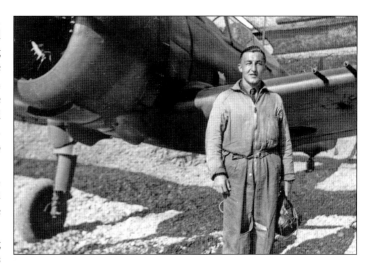

Adj Jérémie Bressieux of GC I/5's 2nd *escadrille* was the last French pilot to be awarded a victory in a Hawk 75 when, on 9 November 1942, he was credited with downing a Wildcat from VF-9. This kill took his overall tally to nine destroyed (*J Bressieux*)

Following the Allied landings in North Africa, GC I/4 became a training unit, thus retaining its Hawk 75s (minus their Vichy-French red and yellow stripes) until the summer of 1943. One of the aircraft assigned to the *Groupe* was Hawk 75A-3 N°291 of the 1st *escadrille* (*P Briand*)

Nakuru, but engine defects limited flying. Another future ace in the form of 2Lt Douglas Golding also arrived at this time from No 43 Sqn.

Although the Mohawks were not reliable, at least No 4 Sqn had modern aircraft with which to train. It was also the first SAAF unit to be totally equipped with the Curtiss fighter. The unit continued to work up until embarking for Egypt in September, where it was to gain a fine reputation flying Tomahawks and Kittyhawks. Its Mohawks, however, remained at Nakuru.

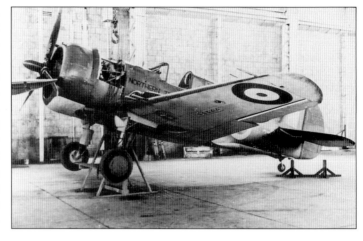

Mohawk IV 2511 was a presentation aircraft named *NORTHERN TRANSVAAL*, and it initially served with No 4 Sqn in Kenya. The aircraft is seen here jacked up for servicing, probably at Nairobi, during the unit's work-up in mid 1941 (*M Schoemann*)

On 13 July 1941, 20 Mohawks with modified engines reached Mombassa from the UK, and by late August they were ready for issuing to units. This proved to be opportune for No 3 Sqn SAAF, as the unit's Hurricanes and Gladiators were in poor shape following the rigours of the campaign in Ethiopia. On 27 August 'B' Flight was re-equipped with Mohawk IVs. However, such was the depleted state of the unit that its element at Alomata was administered by No 41 Sqn SAAF, and 'B' Flight became known for a short time as No 41 Sqn Fighter Detachment.

By now it was apparent to the Allies that Italian transport aircraft were regularly flying re-supply sorties into their stronghold at Gondar using the airfield in the ostensibly neutral Vichy-French colony of Djibouti (in Somaliland) as a staging post. The Mohawk flight led by Capt Hardy Snyman was ordered to move to Aiscia, on the Ethiopian frontier, to try to intercept this traffic, even though its fighters would be few in number.

On 16 September Snyman, with Capt Jack Parsonson and Lt Strong, left for the border on what turned out to be an eventful transit. By the 18th, the detachment was ready at its primitive desert base that was described by Parsonson as 'desert with dry river beds and an arid moon-like landscape unrelieved by any vegetation'. Early the following morning two unidentified aircraft were sighted about 15 miles northeast of Aiscia flying in a southeasterly direction, and Lt Turner took off after them;

This line-up photograph of Mohawk IVs was taken at Nakuru soon after they had been delivered in July 1941. The nearest aircraft was later lost in a crash at Alomata on 20 November, while 2510 parked next to it was flown by future SAAF ace Capt Jack Parsonson. Indeed, he had a minor accident in it on 2 September (*M Schoemann*)

'As I took off they changed course and flew off in the direction of Jibouti. I patrolled in the vicinity where I had seen them but did not see them again.'

As a result of this incursion two line patrols were instigated on the 21st, but the pilots saw nothing. Two days later the detachment received permission to attack the Italians on Vichy territory if required, and patrols along the border continued. These were generally uneventful, although on the 26th Capt Parsonson reported 200 goats moving north

in Area B! The few Mohawks available understandably had difficulty in effectively patrolling the lengthy border, and they were reinforced at the beginning of October when three SAAF Ju 86s and four ancient RAF Vincent biplanes arrived from Aden to assist with the reconnaissance task.

On 4 October the detachment received information that an Italian Savoia transport had landed at Djibouti. Parsonson immediately left to investigate, but in spite of his quick reaction to this news he saw

nothing. The following morning he took off at 0745 hrs in Mohawk IV 2522 and flew another abortive sortie, before returning to Aiscia. After refuelling, Parsonson took off at 1000 hrs and returned to Djibouti, where this time he sighted the Savoia SM.75 parked in the open outside a hangar, as he later described;

'I approached at 10,000 ft, and there stood the Savoia in front of one of the hangars. I decided to attack from the landward side, and then after destroying it I would make my way out to sea. This was my first attack on anything, and I was excited. I circled, put my nose down in a steep dive and made a careful attack. The aircraft loomed large in the sights and I fired a long burst, flashed over it and headed out to sea. I looked back and saw that it was undamaged. I turned for another attack, feeling that this time I must get it. Again it loomed large in my sights as I pressed the trigger – I was very low indeed. As I flashed over it, there was a *whoomph* and it burst into flames. I kept low over the town and turned for home feeling wonderfully elated.'

Parsonson landed 90 minutes after taking off, having destroyed the first aircraft credited to a Mohawk in Commonwealth service – and the only one in Africa. It was Parsonson's first success, and he would later become an ace flying the Kittyhawk in North Africa. Although not noted by Jack Parsonson, the SM.75 was apparently carrying Red Cross markings, having evacuated wounded from Gondar.

On 15 October the detachment officially became 'B' Flight of No 3 Sqn once again, and 48 hours later it was reinforced when two more Mohawks arrived. Patrol tasks then stopped while all the aircraft were thoroughly serviced. On 28 October two Vichy French Potez 63s were spotted taking off during a patrol, but they could not be caught.

While the small detachment at Aiscia was containing Vichy activities at Djibouti, further west, the remainder of No 3 Sqn was supporting the final stages of the campaign in Ethiopia. The main part of the squadron had also received additional Mohawks, and these were used at the start of November for the final preparations for the assault on the Italian fortress at Gondar, north of Lake Tana. The aircraft had been fitted with racks for carrying small bombs, and they joined other RAF and SAAF units in heavy attacks on the demoralised Italians. On the 17th, for example, a dozen Mohawks combined to drop more than five tons of bombs on Ambazzo, Defeccia, Gondar and Azozo.

The only enemy aircraft destroyed by a Mohawk in Africa was Savoia SM.75 I-LUNO, which was strafed on the ground at Djibouti on 5 October 1941 by Capt Jack Parsonson. It had been flying resupply missions into the Italian stronghold at Gondar (*ECPA*)

No 3 Sqn's Capt Jack Parsonson achieved the only SAAF Mohawk victory. He later flew Kittyhawks with Nos 2 and 5 Sqns SAAF, and attained ace status over Tunisia in April 1943. A respected leader, he was shot down attacking a motor torpedo boat soon afterwards and spent the rest of the war as a PoW (*via C F Shores*)

Mohawk IV 2506 served in East Africa with No 3 Sqn, where it performed ground attack missions in the final actions against the Italian fortress stronghold at Gondar (*D Becker*)

The aerial bombardment continued for another ten days until, on the 27th, it had the desired effect when the last Italian fortress in East Africa surrendered. Its capitulation brought to an end the first successful campaign waged by Britain and the Commonwealth against the Axis in World War 2.

After the fall of Gondar, 'A' Flight headed back to South Africa, while 'B' Flight returned to Aiscia. There, on 11 December, a Potez 631 from Djibouti flew over the South African camp at low level, and Lt Gazzard, who had just taken off, gave chase and opened fire. Smoke was seen to come from the port engine before the Potez dived into cloud and vanished. The last SAAF air combat over East Africa saw the only aerial action by a Mohawk in theatre, for which Gazzard was awarded a 'damaged'. The following month 'B' Flight also returned to South Africa.

COASTAL DEFENCE

Throughout 1941, new squadrons were formed in South Africa for service in North Africa. One such unit was No 5 Sqn, which was created in May of that year at Swartkop. Two months after its formation, the unit welcomed leading SAAF ace Maj John Frost as its CO. Several other aces also featured within the ranks of No 5 Sqn at this time, including Capts Andrew Duncan and Robin Pare from the East African campaign.

Initially, the unit's pilots were forced to fly a variety of impressed, obsolete, types. However, following a move to Germiston, it re-equipped with Mohawks, as the squadron's diary entry for 21 October declared;

'Great excitement! Maj Frost, Capts Hewitson and Duncan and two others arrived with five Mohawks, and what a thrill as they roared over the aerodrome faster than anything we have seen. The squadron began to build up the flying activity.'

On the 27th Frost and J L Hewitson flew two Mohawks to Zwartkop, and the squadron followed them on the 31st, when operational training began. This continued on Mohawks until mid December, when orders were received amid much enthusiasm for a move to North Africa. The unit

Mohawk IV 2516/D is thought to have been one of the aircraft detached by No 3 Sqn SAAF to Aiscia, on the Ethiopian frontier, for action against the Vichy French at Djibouti. It is seen here, however, in No 10 Sqn colours following its return to South Africa, having previously served for a short time with No 5 Sqn (*A Jarlski*)

completed its final firing practice with the Curtiss fighter on 12 December and departed soon afterwards. As with other SAAF fighter squadrons that headed into combat in North Africa, No 5 Sqn left its Mohawks in South Africa.

At Zwartkop on 12 January 1942, No 7 Sqn was formed under the command of Maj Doug Loftus, an ace from the desert fighting. Again, the unit was to work up with Mohawks prior to moving to the Middle East. Training began immediately, with an emphasis placed on dogfighting and ground strafing, although engine malfunctions continued to plague the Mohawk. On 5 March pilots were allocated their own aircraft, with Loftus claiming 2501. Two days later, No 7 Sqn began mobility training, moving through Beaufort West and Wingfield, before passing its aircraft on to No 6 Sqn and embarking at Durban for the Middle East.

The outbreak of war against Japan in December 1941 raised the spectre of carrier borne air attacks on South Africa's Indian Ocean coastline – a threat made more real following the successful carrier raids on Ceylon on 5 March 1942. Two weeks later No 6 Sqn was formed at Zwartkop, near Pretoria, under the command of Maj Pieter Hayden-Thomas. He in turn had future ace Maj Laurie Wilmot in charge of flight training, while fellow ace Capt Vernon Lacey became OC 'B' Flight.

In early April 19 Mohawk IVs were transferred from No 7 Sqn following the unit's posting to Egypt, and No 6 Sqn moved to Groutville, in Natal, on the 6th. Five days later four aircraft from 'A' Flight were sent to Stamford Hill, in Durban, where they immediately assumed standby. No 6 Sqn was thus the only SAAF squadron to become operational on the Mohawk in the Union.

On 20 April No 10 Sqn formed under Capt Corry van Vliet as part of the coastal fighter force, but at the end of the month all Mohawks were grounded because of the discovery of white metal chips in the oil filters that had been removed from several engines. Fortunately, this problem proved to be short lived, and in early May No 6 Sqn transferred some of its Mohawks to No 10 Sqn, which in turn sent a detachment to Erste River, near Cape Town.

In spite of these deployments, at 0515 hrs on 20 May, a Yokosuka E14Y1 'Glen' two-seat floatplane that had been launched from the Japanese submarine I-10 overflew the port of Durban without being intercepted. To make matters worse, the aircraft conducted a number of reconnaissance flights over coming days, causing some consternation.

In its defence, No 10 Sqn felt that there were too many delays between detection and the scramble order being received at Erste River. The flights were not without incident or excitement, however. On one occasion, when Lts Sweet and Harrington were returning to Stamford Hill at last light, they were fired upon by a French cruiser that considered them to be hostiles! There was even a report of an unidentified aircraft in the following day's newspapers!

Later that same month No 10 Sqn began its own work-up training on the Mohawk prior to re-equipping with Kittyhawks, which arrived in late June. The following month, the unit transferred its Mohawks back to No 6 Sqn, which remained operational – by then it had come under the command of seven-victory ace Maj 'Bennie' Osler. The unit continued to perform coastal patrols with a variety of types (including the Mohawk) until, with the diminished Japanese threat, it was disbanded on 28 July 1943.

When No 6 Sqn first formed in February 1942, all initial flying training was supervised by the experienced Maj Laurie Wilmot, who later achieved acedom and became a much respected wing leader (*via C F Shores*)

A Mohawk IV of No 10 Sqn sits at readiness, possibly at Groutville, in Natal, in mid 1942 at a time of heightened tension due to the appearance of a submarine-launched Japanese aircraft over Durban (*M Schoemann*)

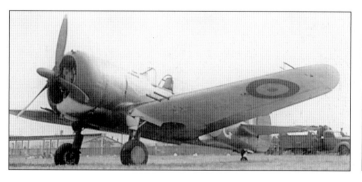

FIGHTING THE SOVIETS

The Winter War that ended on 13 March 1940 resulted in Finland ceding large areas of territory to the Soviet Union, although the Finns did retain their independence. During this brief war, both Britain and France had hastily supplied the Finnish Air Force with fighters and bombers. However, the German invasion of Scandinavia in early April 1940, followed soon afterwards by the fall of France, meant that Britain was in

Finland received a total of seven Wright R-1820 Cyclone-powered Hawk 75A-4s, all of which were initially delivered to reconnaissance squadron LLv 12. CUc-502 of 1/LLv 12 was assigned to flight leader Capt Auvo Maunula, and he is seen here taking off from Joroinen in early July 1941 (*Jussi Laaakso*)

no position to offer any practical support. Thus, Finland was effectively isolated from its supporters in the West, and so only Germany and Italy were left as potential suppliers of military hardware.

The first trade agreement with Germany was signed on 1 October 1940, and it covered the supply of a wide range of military equipment including, among other things, 24 captured MS.406 and 29 Hawk 75A fighters. The latter had been seized from Norway (13) and France (16) and transported by road to Espenlaub Flugzeugbau at Wuppertal, where they were reassembled, fitted with German instrumentation and painted in German colours. The Curtiss fighters were then dismantled once again, packed into crates and shipped to Finland, with 16 arriving during the last week of June 1941 and a further 11 in early August.

The first seven French aircraft to reach Finland were Wright R-1820 Cyclone-engined Hawk 75A-4s, and they received the Finnish Air Force serials CUc-501 to -507. The remaining machines were a mix of Pratt & Whitney R-1830 Twin Wasp-engined Hawk 75A-1s, A-2s and A-3s from France, and 13 A-6s from Norway – the latter bore the serials CUw-551 to -570. The last two Hawks arrived in early December 1941, and they became CU-571 and 572.

Like the RAF, the Finnish Air Force quickly found that the Cyclone-powered Hawk 75A-4s were very unreliable, and these aircraft were duly re-engined with Twin Wasps from 6 December 1941. The 'c' and 'w' suffixes were then dropped from the serials.

CONTINUATION WAR

The German invasion of the Soviet Union, codenamed Operation *Barbarossa*, commenced on 22 June 1941, and it was supported by several nations that bordered the USSR, including Finland – despite Finnish mobilisation only commencing five days before the attack! By then, large numbers of German aircraft were based on airfields in southern Finland in support of operations in the Baltic and the drive on Leningrad.

The presence of Luftwaffe units on Finnish soil quickly became known to the Soviets, who developed plans for a six-day air-offensive from the Arctic Sea to the Baltic. This would involve the Red Air Forces of the Leningrad and Baltic Military Districts and the Northern and Baltic Fleets, which had more than 2500 aircraft available between them, including 900+ bombers and 1300+ fighters. South of the Oulu-Kajaani-Belomorsk frontline, half of this force was directed against Finland.

The first air raids began early on the morning of 25 June, and during the course of the day the Soviets flew 263 bomber and 224 fighter sorties against targets in south and southwestern Finland, after which the Finnish government declared war on the USSR. The Continuation War had begun – and successfully so, as Finnish fighter pilots had claimed 27 bombers shot down on this first day.

When delivered, the Finnish Hawks were at first intended to equip two reconnaissance squadrons, and from 26 June six Cyclone-powered aircraft were delivered to *Lentolaivue* (LLv) 12 to support the Karelian Army north of Lake Ladoga, while eight Twin Wasp Hawk 75As were handed over to LLv 14 for work over the Karelian Isthmus.

Although not an ace on Hawk 75s, Capt Auvo Maunula was a very successful pilot who had flown both the Fokker C.X reconnaissance biplane and the Gladiator fighter during the Winter War. Maunula's first sorties during the Continuation War were made in Hawk 75s in the reconnaissance role. After his squadron received Fokker D.XXI fighters, Maunula was awarded Finland's highest military decoration, the Mannerheim Cross. Eventually, he commanded LLv 12 and, later, LeLv 28 (flying MS.406s), and achieved three confirmed victories.

Although the Cyclone engines quickly proved problematical for LLv 12, the unit still managed to fly 100+ sorties in a fortnight. However, by 10 July it had only two airworthy Hawk 75s available. The Twin Wasp-powered aircraft presented LLv 14 with no such problems. In mid July both units were ordered to pass their Hawk 75s on to LLv 32, based at Utti. All the Finnish Hawk victories would be claimed by this one squadron and, in turn, all but ten of its kills were made on this type.

LLv 32 was part of *Lentorykmentti* (Air Regiment) 3 (LeR 3), and on 12 July 1941 it received a new commander when future ace Maj Olavi Ehrnrooth arrived just as the first Curtiss fighters reached Utti. The squadron was tasked with protecting the Finnish field army, deployed southwest of River Vuoksi, and the industrial areas at Vuoksenlaakso. Both were threatened with attack by Soviet bombers, resulting in the unit flying continuous combat air patrols over these areas.

Opposing LLv 32's Hawks on the Karelian Isthmus was the 5th SAD (Combined Air Division) with its two fighter regiments that flew a mixed force of 223 Polikarpov I-153, I-16s and MiG-3s, while the two assault units had 132 Polikarpov I-15bis biplanes.

LLv 32's Hawk 75 pilots experienced their first success in aerial combat on 16 July when Maj Ehrnrooth, piloting CUw-556, led three fighters against four I-153s in the Nuijamaanjärvi area, shooting one of them down. The kill was shared by Maj Ehrnrooth and future ace WO Eino Koskinen. Several hours later, more Hawk 75s arrived from LLv 12.

Capt Auvo Maunula poses for the camera whilst sat in the cockpit of CUc-502 in July 1941 – 1/LLv 12's emblem, 'Stalin, the Main Devil', decorates the fuselage of his Hawk 75. Twelve months after this photograph was taken, Maunula was awarded the Mannerheim Cross – Finland's highest military decoration. Aside from being an exceptional leader, he also claimed three aerial victories. Maunula commanded fighter squadron LeLv 28 for 21 months prior to being killed in a flying accident on 17 May 1944 (*Jussi Laakso*).

1/LLv 32's leader (and ace) Capt Paavo Berg scrambled in CUw-553 that same afternoon following an attack by ten Baltic Fleet *Chaikas* on Utti. In a brief battle, he shot one down, although Berg was also hit and had to make a forced landing on Lappeenranta airfield. Berg had already 'made ace' during the Winter War, claiming five victories in Gladiators with LLv 26.

Four Hawk 75s were scrambled against *Chaikas* of 7 IAP (Fighter Aviation Regiment) that attacked Utti on 22 July. Fighting over Lake Haukkajärvi, future ace Cpl Mauno

The senior officers of LLv 32 at Lappeenranta on 24 August 1941. They are, from left to right, 3rd Flight leader Capt Aulis Bremer, squadron CO Maj Olavi Ehrnrooth, Hurricane Flight leader Capt Heikki Kalaja, 2nd Flight leader Capt Kullervo Lahtela and 1st Flight leader 1Lt Pentti Nurminen. Behind them is CUw-557, which boasts a tiny sharksmouth on its propeller spinner. All bar Capt Kalaja would subsequently attain ace status (*SA-kuva*)

Kirjonen downed two Russians – the first double kill made by the Hawk 75 – although Kirjonen's CUc-501 was also hit and he baled out.

LLv 32 moved to Lappeenranta on 30 July to support the offensive to retake the Karelian Isthmus, which commenced the next day. The attack initially thrust east of Viipuri under cover of LLv 32's fighters, which were reinforced by 3/LLv 24 to raise the number of available aircraft to 20. LLv 32 flew almost 50 combat air patrols on 1 August over the spearhead of the ground offensive, and it repeated these sorties over the next few days. On 5 August it lost a second Hawk in combat when a trio of machines led by 2/LLv 32's Capt Kullervo Lahtela's fought six I-153s of 7 IAP, which sent CUw-557 down near Nuijamaanjärvi.

Five days later, 1Lt Pentti Nurminen's *schwarm* (four aircraft) of 1/LLv 32 fighters engaged a flight of I-16s over Kirvu, and two Polikarpovs were downed. Future 32-victory ace 2Lt Kyösti Karhila claimed his first kill during this dogfight when he shared an I-16 with fellow future ace 1Lt Veikko Evinen. During the return flight to Utti, the Hawk 75 pilots strafed enemy vehicles, trains and artillery positions.

On 13 August, 1Lt Nurminen's flight of five aircraft from 1/LLv 32 intercepted four *Chaikas* over Antrea and succeeded in destroying three of them in a fierce battle – all the Hawks were hit numerous times during the engagement. The following day, Capt Lahtela's *schwarm* of 2/LLv 32 machines took on a 16 fighters from 7 IAP over the Isthmus at Lenijärvi, destroying two I-16s but losing CUw-561 in return.

Nurminen's flight was again in action on 18 August when 1/LLv 32 (with Brewster 239s of LLv 24's Detachment Karhunen providing top cover) prevented 13 aircraft of 7 IAP from strafing Finnish troops as they crossed the River Vuoksi. The Hawk 75s broke up the Soviet formation and downed four I-153s. Cpl Mauno Kirjonen (in CUw-566) became LeLv 32's first ace during this action, and he subsequently recalled;

'We met one bomber with an escort of about a dozen I-153s. I initially fired a short burst at an I-153, after which I pulled into a cloud. When I came out of the cloud I saw an I-153 diving towards the river crossing area. I went after it and managed to shoot a long burst. The Russian began to pull up whilst I was still firing, and he disappeared into the cloud. I waited, and after a while the I-153 came out in front of me, whereupon

I was able to shoot at it from the side and behind at a distance of 50 m. The fighter went into a dive whilst still on our side of the frontline, and I saw it trailing a flames from the starboard side. I then entered cloud and lost visual contact with my foe.

'Towards the end of the action I saw an aircraft burst into flames and the pilot bale out. The aircraft crashed on the beach at Sintola, next to the road.'

The Hawks found further success on 21 August when Capt Aulis Bremer's patrol from 3/LLv 32 met a *Chaika* flight from 7 IAP above Rautu and downed three of them. An even greater success came 24 hours later when 1Lt Nurminen's *schwarm* shot down three I-153s over Pölläkkälä. On the 23rd Capt Bremer's *schwarm* of 3/LLv 32 machines engaged a five-aeroplane *Chaika* flight in the Suulajärvi area and shot them all down. Future ace Bremer (in CUw-563) recalled;

'At 0945-1030 hrs I attacked the first I-153 with 2Lt Aalto and Sgt Pallasvuo. I fired at it from ahead, in a left bank and from straight behind. After seeing it crash on the north shore of lake Muolaanjärvi, I attacked another. I fired at it from straight behind and also from below, and judging by the tracer rounds, I hit in the fuselage. However, because the combat took place at low altitude deep within enemy territory, I cannot specify where the aircraft crashed. During the battle I observed a few flak explosions, but these were relatively far away from our aeroplanes.'

Bremer only received credit for a solitary kill, as did future ace Sgt Yrjö Pallasvuo (in CUw-564), who also claimed two I-153s destroyed.

Hawk 75 CUw-567 of LLv 32 suffered a right gear leg collapse at Lappeenranta after its pilot inadvertently taxied the fighter into a hole on 26 August 1941. Unlike all other units in the Finnish Air Force, LLv 32 did not allocate individual Hawk 75s to flights, so pilots on duty flew whatever fighter was available at the time, rather than being assigned a personal aircraft (*Reino Lampelto*)

STALEMATE

The advance on the Karelian Isthmus came to a halt on 2 September when Finnish troops arrived at the Red Army's outer defensive lines east of Leningrad. Thereafter, the frontline became fixed for almost three years between the towns of Rajajoki, Valkeasaari, Lempaala and Tappari.

LLv 32's heaviest combat to date in the Continuation War took place on 3 September after Capt Paavo Berg had finished his liaison tour with the ground forces and returned to lead 1/LLv 32. His eight Hawks jumped a *Chaika* squadron over Siestarjoki, and in a 15-minute action the Finns shot down seven of them. 2Lt Kyösti Karhila (in CUw-566), who destroyed one of the I-153s, described the encounter as follows;

'At 1055-1105 hrs, during a surveillance mission, we met six I-153s. I saw one break off towards the sea. I was about 1000 m higher than it, and I easily caught the fighter and latched onto its tail. The pilot was totally unaware of my presence until I opened fire from just 20 m away. The aircraft immediately caught fire and crashed into the sea.'

The Russian losses on 3 September included I-153s from 7 IAP and I-152s from 235 ShAP (Attack Air Regiment).

Three DB-3F bombers from the Baltic Fleet Air Force's 1 AP (Air Regiment) were encountered over Lempaalanjärvi on 15 September by

Capt Kullervo Lahtela's 2/LLv 32. After a short battle, the trio of Soviet aircraft were shot down, as future ace 2Lt Sakari Alapuro (in CU-570) described in his combat report;

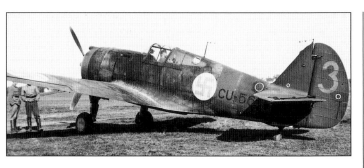

'Whilst patrolling in the Petäjän-mäki area, I spotted three DBs heading north. I attacked one from above and behind in a shallow bank. I quickly silenced the gunner, and the bomber's port engine began to trail black smoke. Due to my higher speed, I had to pull up and pass it. I curved back around again and fired continuously at the starboard engine until it caught fire. The DB then slipped into a cloud. I banked away to the south, waiting for the aircraft to pass through it, but when the DB did not reappear I flew towards Lempaala, where I saw a burning aircraft in a swamp southwest of Rahonjärvi.'

Two days later Capt Berg led a formation of ten Hawk 75s over the frontline, meeting a large number of I-16s above Siestarjoki. One of these was destroyed by 2Lt Karhila, who duly became Finland's first all-Hawk 75 ace on 19 September when he downed a MiG-3 near Ohalatva. This action came as LLv 32 was covering Finnish troops dug in along the frontline and at the crossing points west of River Vuoksi. Karhila was flying one of eight Hawk 75s from 1/LLv 32 that were being led by Capt Berg (in CUw-563). A total of five MiG-3s were encountered, and all of them were destroyed. Berg, who claimed three kills (although he was only credited with two), later recounted;

'Whilst flying at an altitude of about 3000 m, I initially saw four enemy aircraft flying through the clouds in the opposite direction. I made a diving turn and went after them. As I came out of the clouds, I saw an I-17 (MiG-3) just 200 m away. I fired at it and the fighter started smoking and dived away on its back.

'The four Russian fighters that I had previously seen in the clouds were still visible some way away, so I closed up on them and opened fire on the I-17 at the rear of the formation. It dived down to the left and then pulled up again, and I stuck to the aircraft's tail and opened fire. At the same time two more of my pilots (Alppinen and Kajanto) also fired at the now smoking I-17 that I was chasing. I quickly got on the radio and told them that there were more fighters to the left of this one, after which I broke off my attack in order to look for a new target.

'To my left I saw two I-17s flying over the ground at low-level – they both banked to the left and headed southward. I quickly caught the trailing fighter, and when I fired at it, the aircraft began to bank to the left. Turning with my foe, I fired short bursts every now and then, getting closer all the time. I then aimed two bursts ahead of it and the fighter suddenly flicked over to port and crashed. The I-17 was easily caught by the CU.'

The MiG-3s were from 7 and 153 IAPs.

On 21 September Capt Lahtela's flight from 2/LLv 32 was engaged over Ollila by 12 *Chaikas* of 153 IAP, and three were claimed to have been shot down. One fell to WO Koskinen (in CU-558), who recalled;

'After arriving above Terijoki I saw two four-aeroplane patrols of I-153s. At the same time I observed one turning towards me, and I decided

Although not assigned to the senior pilots within LLv 32, CUw-563 was routinely flown by the unit's flight leaders. It is seen seen here between missions at Lappeenranta in September 1941. Note the white rings on the fighter's rear fuselage and tail that denote where bullet holes have been repaired! This machine's Curtiss construction number was 13757, making it a Hawk 75A-3. CUw-563 had been credited with ten victories by the time it was destroyed in a flying accident on 28 June 1942 (*Kullervo Lahtela*)

1/LLv 32 leader Capt Paavo Berg recalls his experiences from a recent dogfight for flight members (and future aces) SSgt Yrjö Pallasvuo and 2Lt Jaakko Hillo at Lappeenranta in September 1941. Berg was already an ace from the Winter War by the time he joined LLv 32, having claimed five kills flying Gladiators (*SA-kuva*)

to attack it from head-on. As I opened fire, the *Chaika* dodged down and I pulled up to the left, whereupon I observed another I-153 in front of me in a banking climb. I managed to shoot at this one from a distance of about 50 m, and watched as it suddenly flipped onto its back and dove away. The I-153 ended up beneath my aircraft, at which point I lost visual contact with it and could not establish whether the fighter had indeed crashed. After this I did not see a single enemy aircraft.'

On 23 September, LLv 32 moved its 15 serviceable Hawk 75s to Suulajärvi, on the Karelian Isthmus. Its next action came on 16 October when Capt Lahtela's 2/LLv 32 scrambled after *Chaikas* had strafed the airfield. The I-153s got away, but two I-16s then tried to attack the base and had the tables turned on them by the already airborne Hawk 75s. A single fighter was downed by Lahtela, taking his tally to four.

For the next 13 days the unit flew a series of uneventful border patrols through to the 29th, when two 2/LLv 32 pilots found a *Chaika* over Ollila. It was swiftly despatched by SSgt Pallasvuo (in CUw-568).

In the wake of the terrible losses it had suffered in the Winter War, the Soviets established a naval and air base on the Hanko peninsula, some 100 kilometres west of Helsinki. Far removed from the fighting surrounding the Finnish offensive towards Leningrad, the Hanko area saw no action until Capt Paavo Berg led the eight-aircraft strong 'Detachment H' to Nummela in late October 1941. The unit had been given the job of neutralising any Soviet aircraft in the Hanko peninsula, which was only a few minutes flying time from Nummela.

Operations commenced on 1 November when Berg and his wingman tried to lure the enemy into combat over Hanko. A solitary I-16 was shot down, but the Finnish Hawk 75s were in turn bounced by more Soviet fighters that were flying as top cover for the lone Polikarpov. Taken completely by surprise, Capt Paavo Berg's fighter (CUw-570) was repeatedly hit and the ace crashed to his death. Capt Kullervo Lahtela was posted in to assume command of 'Detachment H'.

Berg and his wingman had fought Polikarpov fighters from 13 IAP, as was recalled in following extract from the Baltic Fleet journal;

'At 1443 hrs (Moscow time) two I-16 aeroplanes took off from Täktom airfield. They were flown by Lt Gennadiy Tsokolayev and 2Lt Ivan Tvogorov. A short while later, another pair of fighters commenced their take-off run, but Finnish artillery began to shell the airfield and only the I-16 piloted by Lt Vasiliy Golubev managed to get airborne – his wingman had to delay his take-off. Moments later, two I-153s took off, piloted by Lt Aleksandr Ovtsinnikov and 2Lt Grigoriy Semyonov, but they did not participate in the whole combat.

'Two Spitfires attacked Tsoko-layev and his wingman from out of the sun. Tsokolayev dodged with a steep bank and managed to avoid the attack, while Tvogorov's aircraft

CUw-562 of LLv 32 comes in to land at Lappeenranta in September 1941. The black paint on the underside of the starboard wing was applied so that Finnish troops could quickly spot friendly aircraft providing them with air cover during the Karelian Isthmus offensive. This aircraft was lost to ground fire on 24 June 1944 whilst attacking Soviet forces landing at Tuulos, on Lake Ladoga (*Kullervo Lahtela*)

received hits and was damaged. The wounded pilot was able to bring his aircraft back to the airfield, but it broke up on landing. In the meantime, Golubev attacked the Spitfire that had harassed Tsokolayev from out of the sun, and he shot it down. Its destruction was shared between Golubev and Tsokolayev.'

It is apparent from this report that Soviet aircraft recognition had room for improvement!

Four days later, Capt Lahtela's *schwarm* engaged three I-16 fighters of 13 IAP over Tvärminne. Three more Russian aircraft quickly joined them from Hanko, and an I-16 was shot down, as was Hawk 75 CUw-567. The Baltic Fleet journal recorded that I-16 pilots Lt G Tsokolayev and 2Lt D Tatarenko of 13 IAP claimed to have shot down two Spitfires.

Soviet forces evacuated Hanko in late November and 'Detachment H' returned to Suulajärvi on 7 December.

SUURSAARI

On 2 January 1942, the strategically important island of Suursaari (also known as Gogland), in the middle of the Gulf of Finland, was suddenly re-occupied by Soviet troops just a month after they had abandoned it. Six days later, 1Lt Pentti Nurminen's 3/LLv 32 was patrolling over the Karelian Isthmus when the six Hawk 75s intercepted three I-15bis over Lumisuo and claimed all of them shot down.

There was little further action in the area until mid March, when the Finns decided that the ice in the Gulf of Finland was thick enough to support a 'land' assault on Suursaari. 'Detachment Pajari', led by Maj Gen Aaro Pajari, was formed specifically to retake the island, and it was to be supported in this endeavour by LeR 3. Aircraft from the latter unit were to cover the approach of the invasion force as it moved into position on the nearby island of Haapasaari, before commencing its attack on Suursaari itself. Finnish pilots were to also harry retreating Soviet forces.

Pajari's force began its approach on Suursaari on 27 March, with air cover including 13 Hawk 75s from LLv 32. Flying in company with D.XXIs from 1/LLv 30, Capt Bremer's Curtiss *schwarm* from 2/LLv 32 shared in the destruction of an I-153 near Suursaari, and each unit also claimed another fighter apiece.

The Baltic Fleet journal reported that its units flew 58 sorties against the Finns on the 27th as they advanced on Suursaari. Fifteen of these

CU-565 has its engine run up following an overhaul at the field air depot at Immola, prior to being returned to LLv 32 at Suulajärvi on 19 March 1942. It was used to score four and two shared victories. Hawk 75s in the CU-560 to -569 block were marked with yellow tail numbers (*Paavo Saari*)

flights had to be aborted due to snowfall and poor visibility, and an I-16 from 71 IAP, piloted by 2Lt Aleksandr Komelyagin, crashed on the ice. The journal also chronicled an encounter between the Hawk 75s and a formation of four I-16s;

'At 1825 hrs, six enemy fighters attacked four I-16s from 4 GIAP (Guards Fighter Aviation Regiment) at tree-top level. The aircraft of Capt Vasily Zharnikov was shot down in flames near Suursaari, but the pilot was not injured. The I-16 of MSgt Sanin did not return from this mission.'

The phrase 'tree-top level' is an odd one, since all the flying was performed over the vast frozen wastes of the Gulf of Finland!

On 28 March Maj Ehrnrooth led six Hawk 75s against a formation of 20 Soviet fighters flying in two formations. The Finns claimed two *Chaikas* and an I-16 destroyed, with Maj Ehrnrooth (in CU-571) sharing in the destruction of an I-153 to take his tally to five kills.

Suursaari was taken by Finnish troops on the 28th, with LLv 32 providing top cover. Soviet aircraft were conspicuous by their absence until the victorious soldiers commenced their occupation parade late in the day. Prepared for Soviet retaliation, 12 Hawk 75s were providing top cover over the island when 29 Soviet fighter were spotted approaching in three formations. In the 20-minute combat that ensued, the Finnish pilots claimed no fewer than 15 fighters shot down without loss.

1Lt Nurminen (in CU-571) downed an I-16 and an I-153 to become the second all-Hawk 75 ace, as he recounted in his combat report;

'Whilst I was leading a flight of six Curtiss fighters in protection of Suursaari, I received a message from Seivästö. I led my flight west of Lavansaari, at which point I was informed by radio that formations of eight and eleven unknown aircraft had been detected at a height of 3000 m west of Suursaari. My formation also climbed to 3000 m, which took us above the clouds. It was at this point that I saw two formations of aircraft, consisting of both I-153s and I-16s, at about 2000 m.

'I carried out an attack on an I-16, getting in three good bursts from close range from the side and behind. The aircraft shed fragments and went down out of control. Moments later I fired at three I-153s from behind, one of which began to drop away trailing smoke. I could not follow it down, however, because the sky was full of I-153s.

'The Russians had no will for fighting, instead wanting to head for St Petersburg and Harjavalta. I did not observe the Russians firing their machine guns, preferring instead to fire their rocket projectiles. The I-16 is an inferior opponent compared with the I-153. The *Chaikas* did not attempt to turn vigorously when under attack, instead resorting to a climbing turn to port or starboard and then heading straight for St Petersburg, obviously extremely low on fuel!'

The Baltic Fleet journal reported the action as follows;

'At 0840 hrs, 12 I-153s from 71 IAP, led by Capt Pyotr Biskup, and

LLv 32 CO Maj Olavi Ehrnrooth runs up the engine of CUw-552 prior to taking off from Suulajärvi on 26 March 1942. There was little action fought on this day, as the Finnish offensive to retake Suursaari did not commence until the 27th. On 28 March Ehrnrooth scored his fifth, and last, victory to 'make ace' whilst flying CU-571. Ehrnrooth's first three kills were achieved in the Winter War when he flew Fiat G.50s and D.XXIs in the defence of the State Aircraft Factory at Tampere, despite actually being a test pilot at the time (*Aulis Bremer*)

six I-16s from 11 IAP had just finished strafing enemy troops when 15 Messerschmitts and eight Fokkers attacked from an altitude of 1000 metres. Sgt Vasiliy Fyodorov, who fought alone with eight Fokkers, had to make a forced landing near Lavansaari after running out of fuel. The aircraft flipped on its back, but the pilot was not injured. Observation points at Seiskari and Lavansaari reported three Fokkers and a PZL.24 down.

'At 1900 hrs (Moscow time), nine I-153s, led by 71 IAP commander Lt Col Aleksei Koronets,

Eleven Hawk 75 pilots from LLv 32 claimed 15 kills in one combat mission on 28 March 1942 during the Suursaari offensive. Most of them are seen here standing in front of CU-571 at Suulajärvi on 29 April 1942. They are, from left to right, WO Eino Koskinen, SSgt Lauri Jutila, 1Lt Pentti Nurminen, MSgt Mauno Fräntilä, 1Lt Jarl Arnkil, Sgt Aimo Gerdt, 2Lt Sakari Alapuro and Sgt Jaakko Kajanto (*SA-kuva*)

were attacked by nine Fokker and two Curtiss fighters during a ground attack mission eight kilometres north of Suursaari. The escort detachment made a frontal attack and Koronets was killed in the engagement. The I-153s of the strike detachment then joined in the combat after dropping their bombs on the ice. A series of individual clashes were fought that lasted for ten minutes, and Grigoriy Shakbaz shot down a Fokker. He did not return from the mission, however.'

According to this report, 11 IAP stated that it had lost just one I-16 and 71 IAP four *Chaikas* in aerial combat with the Fokkers and 'Messerschmitts' – and all of these fell before noon. There was little mention of the largest air battle of the day fought just before 1900 hrs, when the Finns claimed 15 victories. In addition to what is detailed above, the journal also states that a pilot by the name of Solovyov claimed one individual and one group victory over the 'Messerschmitts'. It appears that a censor has erased some of the less successful events of the day from this chronicle, which was published in late 1945.

On 3 April eight Hawks from Capt Lahtela's 1/LLv 32 flew a reconnaissance mission over the Gulf of Finland. The aircraft were attacked by eight *Chaikas* in the Seiskari area, and five of the latter were claimed destroyed by the Finns. One of these was credited to Lahtela himself, giving him his fifth victory and making him the third all-Hawk 75 ace. The Russians in turn shot down CU-572. This action was also described, rather fancifully, in the Baltic Fleet journal;

'At 1824 hrs a 15-minute combat commenced at a height of just 500 metres between 1Lt Baturin's eight I-153s from 71 IAP and twelve Fokkers (actually Hawk 75s). After the attack by the Soviets, the enemy tried to escape into nearby cloud cover. Those that got separated – obviously less experienced pilots – from the main formation aimed to form up into pairs and *schwarms*, after which they returned to the battle just under the clouds. The more experienced pilots attacked straight out of the clouds.

'The Soviets avoided the surprise attacks and manoeuvred 200-250 metres below the clouds. Three enemy aircraft were shot down in the vicinity of Seiskari and one broke off towards Koivisto. After the combat the enemy fighters broke off to the north. There were no Soviet losses.'

The Finnish Hawk 75s fought their last major air battle over the Karelian Isthmus on 7 April, after which the area fell quiet for more than three months. Flying over Lumisuo on that date, Capt Bremer's 2/LLv 32 engaged ten I-16s and claimed six of them shot down. Bremer (in CU-556) lodged the following combat report upon his return to base;

'At 1520-1600 hrs, I led four aircraft on a reconnaissance mission over the frontline. North of Lempaalanjärvi, I initially observed three I-16s curving around at the edge of a cloud some 1000 m above us. As I climbed up towards them, I noticed that there were at least ten more I-16s 1000-2000 m above the first three fighters cruising along the top of a cloud bank. A long-lasting combat against a superior enemy ensued. I finally got in behind an I-16, and from a distance of 50 metres I managed to shoot straight at it from the side and behind. It quickly began to smoke and crashed at Pieni Suojala, northwest of Lumisuo.

'I shot at another I-16, first from below and then from behind, and then I followed this up with a long and well aimed burst into the engine and cockpit from the opposite direction. After this second pass at the fighter I could not see the I-16 anywhere, in spite of me searching for it, so obviously it had crashed – I later received confirmation of this.

'When the combat began, we were at low altitude due to the fact that we were flying a reconnaissance mission. This meant that we started the engagement with the I-16s from a tactically weaker position than our foes. As the action progressed, we steadily climbed higher and higher. Friendly flak initially interrupted the combat, with well aimed, concentrated bursts exploding all around our aeroplanes. My aircraft was hit three times by shrapnel, which punctured the starboard tyre.'

Both Bremer and Koskinen were credited with two I-16s apiece following this one-sided action, and these kills made them Hawk 75 aces.

A NEW FRONT

With the land fronts having remained generally quiet from September 1941 through to the spring of the following year because of the severe winter weather, senior staff officers within the Finnish Air Force took the opportunity to implement plans for a radical reorganisation in the way fighter units would be employed from now on. Changes were made in order to improve the country's area defence system, although air regiment commanders 'in the field' felt that the new strategy would see their units losing an element of combat flexibility – the main tactical advantage employed so effectively by Finnish fighter pilots to date.

Nevertheless, on 3 May 1942 the front was divided up into three sectors, with a single regiment then being given the responsibility of defending the airspace within that particular sector.

LeLv 32 (the abbreviation of *Lentolaivue* changed from LLv to LeLv at this time too), which had been assigned to LeR 3 on the Karelian Isthmus, was transferred to LeR 1. The latter regiment was charged with protecting the Olonets Isthmus, and its adjacent waterways. LeLv 32 now had to perform all visual reconnaissance, interception and escort duties for the entire regiment within its sector of the Olonets Isthmus.

Prior to leaving LeR 3 for LeR 1, LeLv 32 had claimed 100 aerial victories (between 16 July 1941 and 7 April 1942) for the loss of just six Hawk 75s and five pilots killed in action.

The spring thaw coincided with LeLv 32's arrival at Nurmoila towards the end of May, the unit bringing with it a dozen serviceable Hawk 75s. The Curtiss fighters were in action from virtually the word go, although their immediate opponents overhead the Olonets Isthmus were not large in number. The Soviet's 7th Detached Army was supported by just two fighter regiments, namely 415 and 524 IAPs, sharing just 18 serviceable MiG-3s, LaGG-3s, I-16s and I-153s between them. These aircraft were charged with protecting a bomber regiment and a reconnaissance squadron, both of which were equipped with Petlyakov Pe-2s.

The latter would use their high speed to frequently fly over the western Olonets Isthmus when attacking targets further inland, and the Finns decided to put a stop to this. However, LeLv 32's Hawk 75s proved to be too slow to hunt down the Pe-2s, whose crews often escaped by simply opening the throttles when Finnish fighters were spotted. Indeed, the only time that LeLv 32 managed to engage these aircraft was through employing a height advantage or taking the bombers by surprise.

The first action between the unit and Soviet aircraft occurred over the mouth of the River Svir on 7 June, when a pair of 1/LeLv 32 aircraft claimed two MiG-3s destroyed. One of the latter fell to 2Lt Jaakko Hillo (in CU-503), this success taking his tally to five kills in the Hawk 75 and giving LeR 1 its first aerial victory. Many more were to follow.

Eight days later, a *schwarm* of 1/LeLv 32 machines led by 2Lt Sakari Alapuro bounced four 'Yak-1s' (there were no Yakovlev fighters in this sector, so they must have been LaGG-3s) as they were preparing to land at Mergino, which was the primary Soviet airfield in the area. The Hawk 75 pilots shot two of the fighters down before hastily fleeing the area.

Hawk 75 CUw-555 of LLv 32 is serviced in the open at Immola. Maj Ehrnrooth flew the machine back to Suulajärvi on 4 May 1942 following the completion of this overhaul. 2Lt Kalevi Tervo claimed three of the five and two shared victories credited to CUw-555. Aircraft in the CU-551 to -559 block had white tail numbers (*Paavo Saari*)

CUw-556, seen here at Nurmoila in June 1942, had the construction number 12938, making it a Hawk 75A-2. The fighter was used to claim 11 kills with the Finnish Air Force. During its time with the *l'Armée de l'Air* in June 1940, it had briefly been assigned to future ace Sous-Lt Jan Zumbach, although he did not make any claims with it (*Aulis Bremer*)

The squadron flew 33 sorties on 16 June, and during the course of one of the missions a pair of 2/LeLv 32 aircraft led by 2Lt Kalevi Tervo engaged six LaGG-3s over Mäkräjärvi. One was shot down and the others tried to escape, but a second Soviet fighter was destroyed before the higher speed of the LaGGs saw them flee the pursuing Curtiss pilots.

On the 23rd, 3/LeLv 32's Capt Nurminen and his wingman engaged a solitary U-2 artillery fire control aircraft from 716 AP over Lotinanpelto and sent it down in flames.

The following day, the Hawk 75 pilots finally destroyed a Pe-2 after several weeks of trying. Several of the fast reconnaissance-bombers had been damaged over Olonets Isthmus during the course of the previous week, and it fell to 1Lt Aimo Euramo of 2/LeLv 32 (in CU-571) to finally bring one down. On 25 June six Pe-2s, escorted by two LaGG-3s from 524 IAP, bombed Nurmoila airfield. 2/LeLv 32's 2Lt Kalevi Tervo and his wingman were scrambled to intercept the Soviet aircraft, and although the bombers escaped, the Finnish pilots succeeded in shooting down one of the fighters. Both men enjoyed more success 24 hours later when they destroyed a Pe-2 in the vicinity of Mergino airfield.

Another Pe-2 was brought down on 28 June by 2Lt Karhila and his wingman from 1/LeLv 32 when they intercepted a bomber over the shoreline of Lake Ladoga. The aircraft crashed into the mouth of the River Svir after both of its engines were set on fire.

The Soviets returned to Nurmoila on 5 July, when small formations of aircraft dropped burning naphtha and phosphorus bombs. Several Hawk 75 pilots managed to scramble in defence of the airfield, and they fought a series of running battles with Pe-2s and escorting LaGG-3s. 2Lt Tervo (in CU-560) of 2/LeLv 32 took his tally to 4.5 kills after being credited with two victories, which he described in the following combat report;

'At 1130 hrs, whilst on an intercept mission over Lake Mulevskaya at a height of 4000 m, I observed an aircraft heading south some 2000 m below me. Pushing over into a dive, I soon recognised that the aircraft was in fact a Pe-2. From a distance of about 75 m, I fired my first burst at the bomber's fuselage. Closing to 30 m, I aimed my second burst at its port engine. In the middle of the latter burst, thick smoke started to pour out of the engine and it exploded. The Pe-2 flipped over onto its port wing and crashed in swampy terrain.

'Just as I was about to head back in the direction of Nurmoila, I suddenly saw tracer rounds passing obliquely below and behind my aircraft from the right. Quickly looking over my shoulder, I observed two LaGG-3s flying one behind the other. Pulling my fighter hard into a tight banking turn, I succeeded in getting in behind one of them and fired a short burst at it. The LaGG-3's engine immediately began to smoke and the fighter dropped away to the southwest. In the meantime, the other LaGG-3 had tried to get

CUw-560 under the cover of fir trees at LLv 32's Suulajärvi base in late April 1942. An ex-Norwegian Hawk 75A-6 bearing the construction number 13644, it was also the top scoring Curtiss fighter in the Finnish Air Force with 18 and three shared victories to its credit. CUw-560 was frequently flown by 2Lt Kyösti Karhila, who claimed eight of his 12 and 1 shared kills whilst flying it (*Paavo Saari*)

onto my tail, and its pilot fired two bursts at me, which passed down the port side of my fighter. Seconds later I dived down to the deck and broke off the battle. I did not see whether the LaGG-3 that I had hit crashed.'

Two days later, whilst patrolling near Lotinanpelto, Capt Bremer and WO Koskinen from 2/LeLv 32 intercepted two Pe-2s and their solitary, aggressively flown, LaGG-3 escort. Bremer (in CU-552) recalled;

'As we flew over the River Svir at a height of 3000 m, I spotted three small dots on the horizon. As we got closer to them, Koskinen and I identified the dots as two Pe-2s and one LaGG-3. They turned towards us when we got to within a 1000 m of them. Singling out one of the Pe-2s, I tried to get onto its tail. As I did so, the LaGG-3 turned into me. Ignoring the bomber, I fired a short burst at the fighter from ahead and below. I then turned too tightly in an attempt to get behind the LaGG-3 and briefly lost control of my aircraft. I managed to level it out without losing too much altitude, however.

'In the meantime, the LaGG-3 had attacked WO Koskinen, but he had managed to avoid being shot down. The Russian pilot now went after me again, heading towards my fighter from the port side, shooting all the time. But I was in no danger, as he was aiming too low with too much deflection. I curved in behind the LaGG-3 and closed to within 50 m of its tail, before firing a good burst. Despite it leaving a trail of smoke in its wake, the pilot still made a few shallow turns in both directions. I kept it solidly in my gunsight and continued to fire at it until I ran out of ammunition. The fighter eventually crashed into a forest within enemy territory southwest of Lotinanpelto.'

On 19 July, whilst escorting a Fokker C.X on an artillery fire control sortie over the River Svir, SSgt Paul Salminen and his wingman from 2/LeLv 32 prevented an attack by four I-16s from 524 IAP near Pasha airfield. Three of the Polikarpovs were shot down, with Sgt Väinö Virtanen (in CU-552) claiming two of them to give him ace status.

The next day, 1Lt Veikko Evinen's *schwarm* from 1/LeLv 32 escorted another artillery fire control aircraft, and it too was attacked as it flew over Krestnojärvi. A mixed formation of five LaGG-3s and MiG-3s attempted to shoot the Fokker C.X down, but a single example of each was in turn destroyed. The Finns lost Hawk 75A-4 CU-504 when it burst into flames upon landing back at Nurmoila, the fighter's fuel tanks having been punctured by enemy fire during the course of the engagement.

On the 21st, WO Viljo Ikonen and his wingman from 1/LeLv 32 intercepted five LaGG-3s over the River Svir, one of which was destroyed and the other damaged. Claiming a share in the destruction of the Soviet fighter, SSgt Niilo Erk-inheimo (in CU-558) took his tally in the Hawk 75 to five.

A more unusual Soviet type was encountered by 1/LeLv 32 on 25 July, when the Hawk 75 pilots spotted three MBR-2 flying boats of the Baltic Fleet. The one-sided melee that ensued was described by flight

Eleven-victory ace WO Eino Koskinen poses for the camera whilst sat in the cockpit of LeLv 32's Hawk 75A-3 CU-552 at Nurmoila in June 1942. This aircraft was used to score 14.5 victories, a third of which were credited to 1Lt Kalevi Tervo. During its brief career with the Finnish Air Force, CU-552 suffered three forced landings after its pilots ran out of fuel (*Aulis Bremer*)

CU-504 of LeLv 32 was shot up by Soviet fighters in combat on 20 July 1942 and burst into flames shortly after Sgt Aaro Kiljunen had landed at Nurmoila – the future ace had claimed a MiG-3 destroyed during this engagement. Despite copious amounts of sand being hastily shovelled onto the burning fighter, it could not be saved. CU-504 (construction number 13829) was also an ex-French Hawk 75A-4 – it had been re-engined seven months prior to suffering its fiery fate (*Kullervo Lahtela*)

CU-503 of LeLv 32 flies over the Olonets Isthmus during the summer of 1942. Also an ex-French Hawk 75A-4 (construction number 13816), it too had been fitted with a Twin Wasp engine in March 1942. Ten aerial victories were credited to this fighter, whose individual marking was a red propeller spinner (*Jyri Sarasto*)

leader Capt Kullervo Lahtela (in CU-552);

'Soon after taking off to intercept three unidentified aircraft, I spotted the flak batteries at Olonets firing vigorously, and soon observed three MBR-2 flying boats heading from Olonets to Nurmoila at a height of 200 m. When Sgt Erkinheimo and I attacked these aircraft from behind, the flying boat to the left of the formation broke away to port. Moments later, WO Ikonen shot an MBR-2 down into the forest some five kilometres southeast of the base.

'I went after the flying boat that had turned away to the left, while WO Ikonen and Sgt Erkinheimo remained behind the MBR-2 that was heading east. Sgt Kiljunen and I took it in turns to fire at the aeroplane, stopping any return fire from the crew and causing its engine to trail smoke. It also crashed in the forest. I then returned to base with Sgt Kiljunen, as the third MBR had been set upon by two other CUs.'

The small force of Finnish Hawk 75s next saw action in mid August when, on the 13th, 2Lt Tervo's *schwarm* from 2/LeLv 32 was attacked by four MiG-3s from 524 IAP over Lotinanpelto. In a turning fight, which played into the hands of the pilots flying the nimble Hawk 75s, the Soviets three fighters. One fell to Tervo's guns, thus making him an ace.

Another Hawk 75 pilot reached this coveted status on the 24th when Capt Bremer's *schwarm* from 2/LeLv 32 fought a fierce engagement with 20 MiG-3s. Three were shot down and three more damaged, with 2Lt Yrjö Pallasvuo (in CU-554) claiming a kill to take his overall tally to five.

Soviet fighter pilots now seemed to be more willing to scrap with their Finnish counterparts thanks to the arrival of modern aircraft in the form of the MiG-3 and LaGG-3. Keen to take advantage of this, LeR 1 devised a ruse that it hoped would see a large number of enemy fighters shot down. Vulnerable reconnaissance D.XXIs from LeLv 12 were to be used to lure pilots across to the Finnish side of the River Svir on 9 September.

However, a solitary Pe-2 that just happened to fly through the area at midday triggered the ambush too soon, thus resulting in the Hawk 75 pilots engaging up to 40 Soviet fighters over enemy territory. Despite being hugely outnumbered, the Finns claimed the Pe-2 and ten fighters destroyed, with a further seven aircraft damaged. MSgt Paul Salminen (in CUw-558) shot down two I-16s and a LaGG-3 to become an ace, as he recalled in his combat report;

'WO Koskinen and I engaged a Pe-2, escorted by four LaGG-3s, over Lotinanpelto. I went after the

bomber, but my machine guns did not work properly. Whilst attempting to cock my weapons I lost contact with the enemy aeroplanes. I flew south of the River Svir, where I met 2Lt Tervo. Moments later we both spotted the Pe-2 heading south. We attempted to chase it down, but the bomber was flying too fast for us to get within firing range of it.

'2Lt Tervo broke off the chase and dived for the deck, at which point I saw four LaGG-3s and an I-16 heading for us from above. I began turning into them, and thanks to the Curtiss' unmatched manoeuvrability, I soon had several of the LaGG-3s in my sights. The Russians were firing at me continuously, but very inaccurately, throughout this turning fight.

'I noticed one LaGG-3 attempt to dive away, so I followed it, firing intermittently as we headed for the ground. The pilot levelled off on the deck and I managed to shoot at him from a distance of about 50 m. A few moments later the LaGG-3 crashed into the forest ten kilometres north of Mergino. I then climbed back up to 2000 m and engaged three LaGG-3s and two MiG-3s. Taking one LaGG-3 by surprise, I got onto its tail and shot at it from 50 m. At the same time, three more fighters were firing at me. I was forced to throw my aircraft around in an attempt to lose my attackers, but I also lost sight of the LaGG-3 that I had bounced.

'Having kept my CU in a tight banking turn for as long as was physically possible, firing occasional short bursts at my enemies, I broke off the fight by diving through cloud and heading for the deck. I then flew back along the River Svir, before climbing back up to 2000 m.

'Looking around for further action, I spotted a single CU being chased by three I-16s and a MiG-3 some distance below me. Keen to help my squadronmate, I immediately dived and opened fire at the I-16 that was closest to the CU. The Polikarpov burst into flames within seconds of me opening fire and crashed into the River Svir west of Lotinanpelto. I then went after another I-16, closing to within 30 m of its tail before hitting it hard. The fighter's engine immediately stopped, forcing me to take violent evasive action to avoid ramming it. Nevertheless, the I-16's starboard wing took off my port-side antenna wire. The aeroplane crashed in the forest five kilometres east of Lotinanpelto.

'Climbing for altitude once again and heading east, I saw yet another CU below me being pursued by an I-16. Diving down, I attacked the enemy fighter from behind and then in a banking turn. We were then targeted by fierce flak and my engine was hit, causing it to emit a thick trail of black smoke. Forced to break off my attack on the I-16, I immediately returned to base. The I-16 fled south.'

Ex-Norwegian Hawk 75A-6 CUw-558 (construction number 13660) was one of the top scoring airframes in LeLv 32. Seen here at a sunny Nurmoila on 2 August 1942, it was credited with 17 victories – five of these were scored by Sgt Niilo Erkinheimo. CUw-558's career in the frontline ended on 7 January 1943 when it was hit by an incendiary bomb (*Finnish Air Force*)

Aces Sgt Väinö Virtanen, WO Eino Koskinen, Sgt Niilo Erkinheimo and 2Lt Kalevi Tervo of LeLv 32 check their patrol line on a flight map at Nurmoila in late August 1942. All four pilots had achieved ace status in previous months, with Tervo becoming the newest member of this elite group on 13 August (*SA-kuva*)

Hawk 75A-2 CUw-551 (construction number 13013) was shot up by Soviet fighters whilst escorting a Blenheim IV that had been sent to attack Mergino on 15 September 1942. 2/LeLv 32 ace WO Eino Koskinen nursed the machine back to Nurmoila, where he carried out a near-perfect belly landing. The fighter was credited with 10.5 victories, 3.5 of which were claimed by Koskinen on 5 September 1942 (*Aulis Bremer*)

More action took place on 11 September, despite the weather being overcast and wet. Dodging the showers, LeLv 32 twice sent pairs of Hawk 75s off to intercept incoming Soviet aircraft. Two LaGG-3s from 524 IAP were reportedly damaged in the River Svir area, although one of these was subsequently confirmed as a victory for 2Lt Tervo (in CU-554), giving him ace status.

Four days later, 2Lt Tervo's *schwarm* from 2/LeLv 32 escorted a Blenheim IV sent to bomb Mergino. The aircraft were attacked by a mixed formation of enemy fighters, and the Finns destroyed a LaGG-3 and a MiG-3. On 29 September, 2Lt Karhila and his wingman from 1/LeLv 32 were scrambled after a Pe-2 that had just bombed Nurmoila airfield. It was eventually caught over Saarimäki after the pilot had throttled his engines back to cruising speed, thinking that he was safe from interception. Using cloud cover, the Hawk 75 pilots bounced the Pe-2 and shot it down.

On the last day of September 2Lt Tervo (in CU-552) also managed to intercept a Pe 2, as he recalled in his combat report;

'Scrambled at 1105 hrs following a report that an enemy aircraft had been detected over our lines, I spotted a Pe-2 near Vonozero at an altitude of 4000 m. It flew north-to-east across my flight path, and when I tried to cut it off, the bomber banked first to the east and then headed directly north. Again, as I tried to close to firing distance, it turned back south. This time I got to within 300 m of the Pe-2 as it passed below me, and I fired from ahead and from the rear. The bomber lost speed and went into a gentle descending glide, which meant that I could easily follow it. Shooting continuously at both sides of the aircraft from close range, the Pe-2's port engine soon started to smoke heavily. By then I had only one operable machine gun, so I stopped firing and simply followed the Pe-2 down. The bomber crashed into the forest whilst still in a shallow dive, bursting into flames when it hit the ground.'

The onset of the autumn rains saw the level of aerial combat markedly decrease in October. Indeed, the next action of note did not occur until 7 November, when Capt Nurminen's 3/LeLv 32 escorted a Fokker C.X over the front. A MiG-3 *schwarm* from 415 IAP tried to down the elderly biplane, but all four Soviet aircraft fell victim to the Fokker's fighter escort instead. SSgt Aimo Gerdt (in CU-503) became on ace following

his successes during this mission, as his combat report recalled;

'Whilst performing an escort mission during the early afternoon of 7 November, we were attacked east of Lotinanpelto by two MiG-1s (actually MiG-3s). I got behind the lead aeroplane as it tried to escape towards Savijärvi. Opening fire from a distance of 200 m, the fighter burst into flames and the pilot baled out over Lyugovitsa. This action occurred at 1500 metres.

'I then headed for Savijärvi at a height of 1000 metres, and soon spotted a MiG-1 diving at me from my port side. It attempted to get behind me, but I banked sharply to port and we then completed a tight 360-degree turn. Closing on the fighter's tail, I managed to shoot straight into its cockpit from behind and to the port side. The MiG-1 rolled onto its back and sparks shot out from just aft of its engine. The fighter dived down to the deck southeast of Lyugovitsa, and although I could easily stay behind it as it turned, I was forced to break off my pursuit as it fled further into Russian territory.'

Two days later, whilst reconnoitring Lotinanpelto, 1Lt Tervo's *schwarm* from 2/LeLv 32 intercepted a single Pe-2 from 119 RAE (Reconnaissance Aviation Squadron) and shot it down. The *schwarm* also bounced a section of MiG-3s and claimed two of them destroyed shortly after downing the Pe-2. Tervo was in action again on the 11th when he led his section against a formation of six MiG-3s over the Olonets Isthmus, sending one down in Vonozero area. Three days later Tervo and his wingman attacked an MBR-2 flying boat, which subsequently force-landed at Monastirskaya. These successes were the last credited to 2Lt Kalevi Tervo during his time with LeLv 32, and they took his Hawk 75 tally to 14.25 kills. This score made him the ranking Finnish ace in the Curtiss fighter.

By year-end LeLv 32's increasingly obsolete Hawk 75s had claimed 65 aircraft shot down since the unit had moved to the Olonets Isthmus. Not a single Curtiss fighter had been lost in action during this period, although CU-504 had been destroyed by fire upon its return to base.

2Lt Kalevi Tervo of 2/LeLv 32 prepares to taxi out at the start of yet another mission in the summer of 1942. A cadet officer, Tervo was the most successful Hawk 75 pilot in the Finnish Air Force in terms of aerial victories, being credited with 14 and 3 shared kills. He went on to claim a further six victories with the Bf 109G prior to being killed in action on 20 August 1943. Tervo's final tally stood at 21 and 1 shared victories from roughly 150 missions (*Aulis Bremer*)

NEW LEADERS

Despite the Hawk 75 now beginning to show its age, the Finnish Air Force was able to keep it in frontline service in the Olonets into 1943 due to the modest level of fighter opposition in this theatre.

On 20 January 1943, LeLv 32's CO, Maj Olavi Ehrnrooth, was replaced by Maj Lauri Bremer. A number of experienced leaders subsequently followed their old commanding officer to LeLv 34, which had just been formed to operate the first Bf 109Gs to reach Finland. Amongst those pilots transferred were six aces, namely 1Lt Kalevi Tervo, 2Lts Kyösti Karhila, Mauno Kirjonen and Yrjö Pallasvuo, plus SSgts Niilo Erkinheimo and Aimo Gerdt.

The last of these aces to claim a Hawk 75 kill was Kyösti Karhila (in CU-560), who took his final tally to 12.25 victories on 11 February. His combat report read as follows;

'Whilst on a late morning patrol with 1Lt Arnkil, WO Ikonen and Sgt Kiljunen, I observed an aircraft over Lyugovitsa at about 3500 m performing vertical turns. I radioed this information to WO Ikonen and his wingman, Sgt Kiljunen, as they were closer to the aeroplane both in terms of height and distance. I then saw Ikonen attack the aircraft, which dove underneath him, then made a half roll and continued straight on into a vertical dive. It was at this point that the pilot baled out, although I did not observe a parachute opening. The aircraft crashed into the forest some five kilometres southeast of Saarentaka railway station.

'We joined up once again and then climbed for height as we headed for Lotinanpelto. As we approached the town I spotted two aircraft to the south of the local power station. I got on the radio and told the others to go and take a look at them. They quickly reported that the contacts were in fact friendly aircraft. I then spotted another machine to the south that was a little higher than the first two, and I announced that I was going to intercept the new contact. When I got closer, to the solitary aircraft, I discovered that there were more aeroplanes in this area – one much higher than me that was using the sun to obscure his position and two below me flying as a pair. The latter aircraft were LaGG-3s.

'I dived down on the fighters below me, and they half-rolled away. I focused on the wingman, who tried to climb to safety. Pulling my CU into a tight banking turn, I quickly closed in on the LaGG-3 and eventually opened fire at it from a distance of just 50 m. My tracers hit the aeroplane's engine and it commenced a steep curving turn to the left. Presented with a good deflection shot, I fired. The fighter immediately straightened out and pulled up, and I hit it in the oil cooler. The LaGG-3 burst into flames and went down in an inverted dive near Bolato.

'Shifting my attention to the lead LaGG-3, I got onto its tail and gave the fighter a burst from a distance of 100 m. The pilot pulled up to the left and began turning away from me. I hit it twice more and the aeroplane began to smoke. The fighter dived away to the south and succeeded in leaving me behind due to its greater speed. Sgt Kiljunen then took up the chase, as he had used his greater altitude to build up more speed than me when diving after the LaGG-3. Leaving him to it, I sought out a new opponent.

'A few minutes later I spotted a LaGG-3 below me on my port side heading south. Closing on the fighter, I opened fired from a

2Lt Kyösti Karhila of 1/LeLv 32 was the second highest scoring Hawk 75 ace in Finland, claiming 12 and 1 shared victories. He also became the ranking ace of all Curtiss pilots, increasing his tally to 32 and 1 shared destroyed flying the Bf 109G. By war's end Karhila had flown 304 missions (*Kyösti Karhila*)

distance of about 100 m and kept on firing until I almost collided with the aircraft. I observed my tracer rounds sinking into its fuselage, and also saw that the aircraft's flaps had dropped out.

'Having broken off my attack so as to avoid colliding with the fighter, I saw Sgt Kiljunen also fire at the same aircraft prior to pulling away. Returning for another firing pass, I scored numerous hits on the LaGG-3 from the right side. The aircraft was just 50 m above the ground by this point, and it hit the ice at the northern end of Lake Savijärvi at a 30-degree angle. A cloud of snow shot up as the fighter crashed, and once it had cleared, I saw that the LaGG-3 had travelled some 30 m across the ice and turned some 135 degrees to the left. The wings appeared to have been partially sheared off, with the port one resting almost alongside the fuselage and the starboard wing sticking up at an angle.

'At this point the lead LaGG-3 that I had unsuccessfully attacked earlier in the mission returned to check on the fate of his comrade. Trying to get in behind the aircraft, I initially fired at it, and missed, as we turned tightly into each other. The Soviet pilot then fled south, using the LaGG-3's superior speed in level flight to leave us trailing in his wake.

'As we headed further south, I observed flak bursts a few hundred metres off to our right overhead the Soviet airfield at Novinka. The flak grew heavier as we approached, with the shells being fitted with the shortest possible fuses so as to detonate them at our low altitude. As our fighters began to be buffeted around by the explosions, I yelled "get home, and fast!" over the radio to my pilots. Prior to leaving the area, I spotted two large aircraft, camouflaged in green, parked on the airfield. Sgt Kiljunen and I dove for the deck and flew in the direction of home – there were no enemy aircraft following us.

'As we headed home, I observed a gaudy black and white-striped U-2 biplane flying just above the ground directly ahead of me. I quickly pulled up and shot at the aircraft from behind and above. My tracer rounds hit the fuselage around the cockpit area, and the aeroplane crashed into a forested area at the northern end of Lake Malkjärvi. Its port wings hit a tree and broke off and the aeroplane nosed over.

'We continued the journey home on the deck.'

During the morning of 4 March, a *schwarm* of fighters from 1/LeLv 32 flew an escort mission for a Fokker C.X reconnaissance aircraft. The latter had successfully completed its photo passes and was on its way home when enemy aircraft were spotted. Sgt Aaro Kiljunen (in CU-562) recalled;

'Whilst returning from an FK escort mission with 1Lt Taina, 2Lt Karhila and SSgt Erkinheimo, I observed a Pe-2 and a MiG-3 heading south at a height of 4000 m. We chased them to the eastern side of Mergino but could not catch them. When we turned back, I lost sight of 1Lt Taina, and shortly after that I observed three MiG-3s heading towards me at a little below my

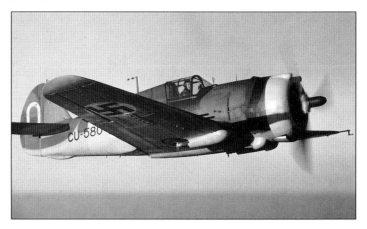

1Lt Jaakko Hillo leads his *schwarm* in ex-French Hawk 75A-2 CU-580 during an escort mission for a Fokker C.X photo-reconnaissance aircraft from LeLv 12 sent to reconnoitre the River Svir on 16 October 1943 (*SA-kuva*)

altitude. I managed to shoot at one of them head-on as we flew by each other. I saw my tracers hit its engine and canopy. With the sun at my back, the Soviet pilot had not spotted me as we came together, and he did not return fire as I closed in on him.

'Following this firing pass, I pulled up to the left and spotted that the aforementioned MiG-3 was diving towards the ground at a 60-degree angle, whilst the other two fighters were climbing up in the direction of the sun. The two surviving MiG-3s then forced me to dodge continuously for a number of minutes as they employed so-called pendulum tactics in a series of attacks. They would take it in turns to make firing passes at me, before pulling up towards the sun. I had to beat a hasty retreat in the direction of Segesjärvi, flying straight and level as fast as I could until the MiG-3s left me alone. I was now low on fuel, so I returned directly to the airfield.'

Kiljunen's MiG-3 kill gave him ace status in the Hawk 75.

RARE COMBAT LOSSES

Having gone months without any combat losses, LeLv 32 suffered two in a single mission on 19 March. A *schwarm* was flying top cover for a Fokker C.X in the central River Svir area when the aircraft (CU-565) of flight leader, and ace, Capt Pentti Nurminen was hit by ground fire. The pilot force-landed in Russian territory and was quickly captured. A second Hawk 75 (CU-554) was also hit by flak, and it crashed between the lines. These would prove to be the only combat losses suffered by LeLv 32 during 1943.

The campaign on the Olonets Isthmus remained stalemated throughout the year, and this in turn meant that there were only occasional encounters between the Finns and their Soviet counterparts in the air. One such engagement took place on 8 July, when 1Lt Jaakko Hillo and his *schwarm* from 3/LeLv 32 intercepted a formation of LaGG-3s during an escort mission over the Lotinanpelto-Alehovtsina sector. One Soviet fighter was shot down and a second damaged.

In order to maintain the viability of its small force of Hawk 75s, Finland had bought a further 15 aircraft from German war booty stocks during the spring of 1943. These were duly collected by Finnish pilots and flown to the State Aircraft Factory for a complete overhaul. The first of these 'new' aircraft was delivered to LeLv 32 on 10 August, and over

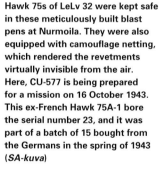

Hawk 75s of LeLv 32 were kept safe in these meticulously built blast pens at Nurmoila. They were also equipped with camouflage netting, which rendered the revetments virtually invisible from the air. Here, CU-577 is being prepared for a mission on 16 October 1943. This ex-French Hawk 75A-1 bore the serial number 23, and it was part of a batch of 15 bought from the Germans in the spring of 1943 (*SA-kuva*)

subsequent weeks seven more were received. This allowed the unit to maintain an average daily strength of 10-12 serviceable Hawk 75s.

2/LeLv 32 suffered a rare loss on 17 November whilst escorting Blenheim IVs sent to bomb Volhovstroi. On the return leg of the mission, 1Lt Mauri Aalto (in CU-506) attempted to fly beneath the bombers but hit one of them and had his rudder badly crushed. The fighter crashed in Olonets Isthmus, killing Aalto, who had four and one shared victories to his name.

Little action came LeLv 32's way during the second half of 1943 and into 1944, with the unit predominantly flying uneventful escort missions for bombers and reconnaissance aircraft.

On 14 February 1944, the abbreviations of the squadrons in the Finnish Air Force received a role prefix, thus *Lentolaivue* 32 became *Hävittäjälentolaivue* 32 (Fighter Squadron 32, abbreviated to HLeLv 32). The squadron had 18 Hawk 75As available, but these were rapidly being outclassed by new La-5s that were reaching Soviet units in the area in growing numbers. Finnish pilots first encountered the new Lavochkin fighters on 24 February, and they proved hard to beat. For example, on 26 March two La-5s bounced a Hawk 75 near Nurmoila and shot it full of holes, wounding 3/HLeLv 32 leader 1Lt Reino Hakulinen.

The spring thaw lasted for the whole of April, rendering airfields too muddy to operate from and preventing the next encounter from taking place until 8 May, when 1Lt Virtalahti's *schwarm* from 3/HLeLv 32 engaged a pair of La-5s from 415 IAP over the western Olonets Isthmus. For once enjoying a numerical advantage, the Finns managed to send one of the potent fighters down. The credit for this victory was split between three pilots, one of whom was WO Eino Koskinen – this would be his last claim, taking his total to 11 and 1 shared kills overall.

By now there were few aces left in HLeLv 32, and the chances of its pilots getting more victories in the Hawk 75 were very limited. Some succeeded, however, including 1Lt Hillo, who led six Curtiss fighters from 1/HLeLv 32 on a bomber escort mission to Mergino on 28 May. They were attacked over the target by 20 La-5s from 415 IAP, and the Finns, whose ranks included a pair of Bf 109Gs on attachment from 1/HLeLv 24, fought back and claimed six enemy fighters shot down for the loss of CU-555.

Almost a month later, on 22 June, a 1/HLeLv 32 *schwarm* led by 1Lt Hillo bounced an Il-2 *Shturmovik* formation over the western Olonets Isthmus and shot down two of the ground attack aircraft near Kuittinen. Both of the unit's remaining aces, Hillo and Kiljunen, shared in the destruction of one of the Il-2s.

The following day the Soviets launched a major offensive in the Olonets Isthmus, forcing the Finnish Army to retreat some 100 kilometres over a three-week period. It was the beginning of the end for the

When the engine of TLeLv 12 D.XXI FR-95 failed on take-off at Nurmoila on 26 February 1944, the aircraft stalled and crashed into the blast pen in which CU-574 was parked. Miraculously, neither aircraft suffered too much damage as a result of the accident. In early 1944, the Hawk 75s of HLeLv 32 had been painted with detachment markings comprising one, two or three white stripes on the fin (*Finnish Air Force*)

Finns, as the Red Army was to prove virtually unstoppable. Following fierce fighting, the communist offensive was finally stopped in August. A negotiated peace treaty was then thrashed out between the protagonists that resulted in a cease-fire commencing on 4 September. A permanent truce was signed a fortnight later.

The Red Army's final offensive had been heavily supported from the air, and this meant that there was no shortage of targets for the Hawk 75s of HLeLv 32. On 28 June, 1Lt Sakari Alapuro led a *schwarm* from 3/HLeLv 32 on a reconnaissance mission over the frontline to ascertain the extent of the enemy advance. As they approached Säntämä, the Finnish pilots were engaged by two LaGG-3s, one of which was shot down into the forest below. This was the fifth claim for Sakari Alapuro, who became the last pilot to 'make ace' whilst flying the Hawk 75.

Three days later, fellow ace 1Lt Jaakko Hillo of 1/HLeLv 32 engaged Il-2s from 839 ShAP (Attack Air Regiment) over Olonets. He and his wingman managed to down one of the attack aircraft, thus taking his final tally to eight and one shared destroyed. Hillo's Il-2 was also the last aircraft to be shot down by an ace whilst flying a P-36/Hawk 75.

Despite the obsolescence of their mounts, Finnish Hawk 75 pilots had still managed to claim two-dozen aerial victories in 1944, thus raising the type's overall score in Finnish service to 190.5 kills. This total was achieved by 30 pilots, half of whom had 'made ace' in the aircraft.

The story of the Curtiss Hawk in Finnish service was not quite over, however. In the peacetime reorganisation of the armed forces on 4 December 1944, all the squadrons were renamed and the Hawk 75s transferred to HLeLvs 11 and 13, both of which were part of LeR 1. Based at Pori, on Finland's west coast, these units continued to fly the aircraft as fighter trainers until 30 August 1948, when CU-560 and CU-578 made the type's last flights in Finnish Air Force service. All surviving aircraft were then put into storage and eventually scrapped in 1953.

CU-559 of HLeLv 32 is seen at Mensuvaara in August 1944. Despite the aircraft's obsolescence as a fighter by this late stage in the war, the Hawk 75s flew numerous missions during the summer campaign. Its excellent manoeuvrability often saved the Curtiss fighter when engaged in combat by the more modern La-5, which was now its primary opponent. The wear and tear inflicted on the Hawk 75s during the bitter fighting of 1944 is clearly visible on this machine (*Kullervo Lahtela*)

After the war, most of the 16 surviving Hawk 75s were assigned to LeR 1 squadrons HLeLvs 11 and 13, although a few examples such CU-560 also found their way to the Air Fighting School at Kauhava. Photographed in the summer of 1947, CU-560 subsequently made the Finnish Air Force's final Hawk 75 flight on 30 August 1948 (*Paavo Saari*)

THE RISING SUN

Shortly after 0600 hrs on 7 December 1941, the first wave of 183 fighters, dive-bombers and torpedo-bombers launched from the aircraft carriers *Akagi, Kaga, Soryu, Hiryu, Shokaku* and *Zuikaku* of the Imperial Japanese Navy (IJN) as the vessels sailed some 200 miles north of the Hawaiian Island of Oahu. The aircraft set a course for the US Navy's main Pacific base at Pearl Harbor. This wave comprised Aichi D3A1 'Val' dive-bombers and Nakajima B5N2 'Kate' level and torpedo-bombers, escorted by 45 Mitsubishi A6M2 Zero-sen fighters that had also been ordered to strafe the various airfields in the immediate area. A second wave of 165 aircraft began taking off 45 minutes after the first one had departed.

At 0755 hrs Japanese aircraft were detected by American spotters to the southeast heading towards Pearl Harbor, and almost immediately Hickam Field and the nearby naval anchorage came under attack. The first wave of IJN aircraft bombed and strafed targets for about 30 minutes. There was a brief lull of 15 minutes before the second wave (consisting of more level and dive-bombers) arrived overhead at 0840 hrs. In Pearl Harbor, battleship row was singled out by the Japanese crews, with USS *Arizona*, USS *California* and USS *West Virginia* all being sunk, and USS *Oklahoma* capsizing. USS *Nevada* had also been badly bombed, and three other capital ships received varying degrees of damage.

At Wheeler Field, the first bombs fell shortly after 0800 hrs, swiftly reducing the base to chaos. Hickam and Bellows Field were also hit, and so effective was the attack that it was virtually impossible to put up anything approaching an effective defence. Nonetheless, at 0835 hrs four P-40Cs and two P-36As took off from Wheeler Field, and for the next hour they flew 25 sorties.

A handful of pilots – some still in their tuxedos following a party the previous night – that were spending the weekend on base at Wheeler desperately drove to Haleiwa auxiliary field, some 15 miles away, where a number of P-40s and P-36s had been temporarily assigned from the 47th PS so that crews could achieve their gunnery qualifications. Due to a shortage of 0.50-in machine guns in Hawaii, the P-36s were fitted with just one nose-mounted 0.30-in machine gun.

At 0830 hrs, two P-40s and four P-36s took off, with one of the latter being flown by 19-year-old 2Lt Harry W Brown. Heading for

Some of the pilots that claimed victories on 7 December 1941 pose for the press the very next day in front of the P-36A said to have been flown by 2Lt Harry Brown when he claimed his two victories. They are, from left to right, 1Lt Lewis Sanders and 2Lt Philip Rasmussen, who flew P-36s and each claimed a Zero destroyed, 2Lts Ken Taylor and George Welch, who were credited with six kills between them flying P-40Bs, and 2Lt Harry Brown, who claimed a pair of B5N 'Kate' torpedo-bombers, although these were initially credited to him as D3A 'Val' dive-bombers (*USAF*)

Wheeler, he soon spotted the P-36 flown by 2Lt Bob Rogers, and they both unsuccessfully attacked a B5N 'Kate'. Brown later recalled;

'I could hear Rogers shouting on the radio but couldn't ascertain what he was saying. I started a slow turn to the right, and suddenly there were three aeroplanes over Kaena Point. I started for them and, as I closed, could see that two Japanese aeroplanes were in hot pursuit of a P-36, presumably flown by Rogers.

'They were slightly below me, and I dove toward the second one. He snap-turned inside me, leaving me almost on the tail of the first one. He made a mistake! He tried to turn away from me and, of course, flew right through my line of fire. I wasn't more than 10-15 ft behind him, and I couldn't have missed. I saw the rear gunner crumple and the left wing begin to burn, so I snapped to the right and climbed to set myself up for another pass. I saw the aeroplane hit the water almost vertically.'

Turning left to look for the second enemy aircraft, Brown was confronted by a dozen others, and he flew right through them! He then dived on a straggler, only to discover that it was yet another P-36 that then jumped one of the enemy bombers. However, the US fighter then broke away, so Harry Brown moved in and had three successful firing passes before his ammunition ran out;

'I know I inflicted heavy damage on my first pass. I saw the pilot's canopy shatter and the engine take some hits. The last time I saw him he was headed out over Kaena Point in the general direction of Kauai, trailing a column of black smoke and rapidly losing altitude.'

2Lt Brown had begun his path to acedom (which he achieved flying P-38s with the 475th Fighter Group over New Guinea in 1943), and he was the only US ace to claim a victory with the P-36. He then returned to Haleiwa, where the other Curtiss fighters had also landed to refuel.

At Wheeler, 1Lt Lewis Sanders (commander of the 46th PS), having managed to save several P-36s and get them prepared for action, led four of them off at 0850 hrs just as the second wave began its attack. One was flown by the pyjama-clad 2Lt Philip Rasmussen, who took off in an all-silver P-36A. Among the other pilots was 2Lt Gordon Sterling, who, in the confusion, had manned 2Lt Norris' aircraft. Having climbed into the aircraft, he took off his watch and handed it to the crew chief, saying 'Give this to my mother. I'm not coming back!'

The P-36A flown by 1Lt Lewis Sanders, commander of the 46th PS, has its starboard undercarriage leg checked and its solitary 0.30-in gun rearmed at Wheeler Field after seeing action against the first attack wave of Japanese aircraft on the morning of 7 December 1941. He was credited with shooting down an A6M Zero-sen during this sortie (*USAF*)

Like those who flew from Haleiwa, most of these pilots had recently passed their gunnery tests, and were therefore better qualified than many of their compatriots in Hawaii at this time.

Climbing hard for the first 20 minutes of the mission in order to gain a height advantage, Sanders then led his small group down onto a formation of enemy fighters. He attacked the leading Zero, which was flown by Lt Fujita, while both 2Lts Thacker and Rasmussen engaged other IJN fighters. Sterling, meanwhile, had got in behind another Zero, but he was soon in serious trouble as Fujita's aircraft appeared on his tail. Seeing his young wingman coming under fire, Lew Sanders, having climbed up and away after his initial skirmish, dived on Fujita but was unable to save the young tyro, as he later described;

'Just as I closed in, he got off a burst at Sterling, whose aeroplane burst into flames. Four of us then went into a dive – the Japanese pilot in front then Sterling, firing at him, then another Japanese and then me. We plunged into the overcast that way. I was some distance behind, and when I came out, there was no sign of the other aeroplanes. The way they had been going, they couldn't have pulled out, so it was obvious that all three went into the sea.'

Both Sanders and the unfortunate Sterling were credited with victories, although both Japanese fighters survived, albeit damaged.

The gallant action by the P-36 quartet was not yet over, however, for 2Lt Thacker experienced a beam attack from a Zero whilst he was flying in circles trying to re-cock his guns. He later recounted;

'A 20 mm explosive shell had fractured my tailwheel hydraulic line. I smelled hydraulic fluid in the cockpit, so I quickly ducked under some clouds and left the scene.'

The Zero, thought to have been flown by PO2c Tanaka, then crossed the nose of 2Lt Rasmussen's P-36;

'I came up on the belly of one and raked it from nose to tail. I did not see the craft I shot actually crash, but he was smoking.'

He claimed the result as 'uncertain', although it was later confirmed as destroyed by US authorities. His elation was short lived, as he continued;

'At almost the same instant I was hit by two 20 mm explosive cannon shells – one, in the radio compartment behind my head, shattered the canopy above me. The other, in the tail section, severed my rudder cable and blew off my tailwheel. In addition, I was stitched with 7.7 mm bullets. Having little control over the aircraft, and scared as hell, I popped into a cloud, struggled to stabilise the P-36 and headed for Wheeler.'

Back at base, future eight-victory ace 2Lt Bill Haney sprinted to the line of P-36s that were being armed. With bombs falling, he managed to get airborne and join Sanders' small group, only to be struck by fire from the heavy cruiser USS *San Francisco*. With his engine knocked out, Haney was forced to make a dead stick landing. Undaunted, he immediately jumped into another P-36 and took off, only to be hit by ground fire once again and forced to land back at Wheeler with a dead engine for the second time in less than an hour!

As the second wave of Japanese aircraft headed back out to sea, seven P-36s and a pair of P-40s took off. The USAAC fighters failed to intercept the IJN formation, however, and flew an uneventful patrol. 2Lt Francis Gabreski was at the controls of one of the P-36s;

2Lt Francis Gabreski was one of a number of future USAAF aces that flew the P-36 in Hawaii. Serving with the 45th PS, he undertook a fruitless defensive sortie on 7 December 1941 shortly after the last wave of IJN aircraft had left Hawaiian skies (*via W Matusiak*)

Mohawk IV BJ546/OQ-O of No 5 Sqn was one of several deployed to Akyab in mid March 1942 and flown by pilots attached to the unit from No 67 Sqn, including successful New Zealander Sgt 'Ketchil' Bargh. BJ546 was lost during a sortie to Fort Hertz on 24 May whilst being flown by Sgt Gordon Campbell (*C V Bargh via C F Shores*)

'We could see tracers arcing up toward us, and occasionally a smoky burst of flak would explode nearby. We continued to search the skies for another 45 minutes, but the Japanese were long gone. We never did receive any orders from the ground, so when our fuel started to get low Capt Tyer led us back to Wheeler.'

Sadly, during his third defensive sortie, 2Lt John Dains was killed by indiscriminate ground fire, thus marking a tragic end to the efforts of the P-36, whose combat career in its homeland had lasted less than an hour.

Those P-36s that remained were quickly replaced, and by the time of the Battle of Midway in June 1942, the 18th PS at Elmendorf had only three examples still on strength. These were probably the last US aircraft that potentially could have seen action against the Japanese, as other USAAF P-36s still serving in the frontline were based in the Canal Zone with the 16th and 32nd PGs, where they experienced no combat.

OVER THE CHINDWIN

As tensions in the Far East rose through 1941, the RAF fighter force in India was in a parlous state, and in the absence of more potent types, a total of 86 ex-French contract Hawk 75A-4s were delivered from October 1941. By the time No 5 Sqn received its first Mohawk IV on 29 December, the Japanese were pushing into Burma and fighters of any sort were desperately needed. By the end of February 1942, the squadron had received 13 Mohawks, and in March it was declared operational at Dum Dum for the defence of the sprawling port of Calcutta, although the lack of an early warning radar system was a handicap.

When remnants of No 67 Sqn arrived at Chittagong, having evacuated from Burma, the unit was ordered to detach a flight to No 5 Sqn. One of the pilots seconded to the latter unit was New Zealander Sgt Vic 'Ketchil' Bargh, who already had two victories and two probables to his credit flying Buffaloes. After the briefest of conversions, four pilots from No 67 Sqn flew down to Akyab in the No 5 Sqn Mohawk IVs on 15 March to provide air defence for this vital port. They had almost no support, as 'Ketchil' Bargh recalled;

'It was silly to send us down. We had to start the aircraft ourselves. We had to sit on the aerodrome down at Akyab and wait. All you could do was look over the hills and hope they didn't come up the coast.'

The No 67 Sqn pilots that were attached to No 5 Sqn in March 1942. On the extreme right is Sgt Bargh, who eventually claimed three victories and two probables over Burma – none in the Mohawk, however (*C V Bargh via C F Shores*)

No 146 Sqn received only a handful of Mohawks, but they did wear unit codes, as shown on this aircraft (believed to be BS788/NA-A) at Tezpur. Battle of Britain ace and unit CO Sqn Ldr Count Manfred Czernin flew this particular machine on 23 April 1942 (*D Linn*)

They were recalled on the 20th just before a series of heavy raids that forced the evacuation of the area. Bargh commented on the Curtiss;

'I thought they were bloody good up to 15,000 ft. I tell you what, they were as good as a Hurricane up to a certain height, but they didn't have enough firepower.'

In early April a Japanese force based around the light carrier *Ryujo* sortied into the Bay of Bengal, creating havoc among coastal shipping. On the morning of 6 April, a convoy was attacked by three Japanese cruisers and their seaplanes. During the course of one of these attacks, a Nakajima E8N2 'Dave' floatplane from the cruiser *Kumano* was attacked by a patrolling No 5 Sqn Mohawk without result.

Two more Mohawks were scrambled, and Flt Lt Keith MacEwan in BS795/QO-W spotted a floatplane as it was about to alight ahead of *Kumano*. Diving down, MacEwan fired and reported that the 'Dave' had ditched in the sea. Lt Itoh's E8N2 had, in fact, alighted with only slight damaged. Nonetheless, the Mohawk had been blooded with the RAF.

In a further effort to bolster India's air defences, No 146 Sqn at Dinjan, in Assam, received a handful of Buffaloes and Mohawks in March 1942 to supplement its thoroughly obsolete Audax biplanes. A new CO also arrived at the end of the month in the form of Battle of Britain ace Sqn Ldr Count Manfred Czernin, who flew his first Mohawk sorties on 5 April. After a familiarisation flight in BS795 during the morning, Czernin (again in BS795) and Flt Lt Ian Aitkens scrambled later that same day following an alert that a Japanese raid was on its way – nothing was seen, however.

Manfred Czernin flew the Mohawk several more times during the month, but such was the shortage of aircraft that in early May they were all concentrated with No 5 Sqn, and No 146 Sqn had to wait for Hurricanes. At Dum Dum, Officer Commanding Flying was another Battle of Britain ace, Wg Cdr Harborne Stephen, who also regularly flew the Mohawk. Unfortunately, on 25 April 1942 he was forced to bale out of a Curtiss fighter following a rapid dive from 10,000 ft which resulted in the oil flowing into the cockpit, and not the engine!

In early May No 5 Sqn moved north to Dinjan to support operations in northern Assam, with a detachment being maintained at Tezpur, on the Brahmaputra River, under the command of Flt Lt Joe Cunliffe. The following month Sqn

Ldr Bill Pitt-Brown became the CO, and he told the author;

'Joe Cunliffe operated down the Chindwin Valley and Imphal while we covered a wide arc from east of Dinjan to Fort Hertz, with Myitky-ina, which had a good airfield, as the main focus. This was the Burma end of the evacuation link to Dinjan, which was operated by a motley collection of transport aircraft. We covered the route as much as possible in terrible monsoon weather.'

On 7 July the unit started flying ground attack missions, although the Mohawks could only carry 20-lb anti-personnel bombs. Four fighters attacked lines at Kalumyo, and the next day Pitt-Brown bombed a railway siding east of Nunti.

Little was seen of the Japanese Army Air Force (JAAF) during this campaign, and it was not until 20 August that No 5 Sqn finally claimed its first confirmed aerial victory, as Sgt Stuart Garnett recalled;

'My section of two Mohawks was returning from Mawlaik at a height of 6000 ft when we sighted a single-engined aircraft at "two o'clock down", flying along a river in the opposite direction to us. The red roundels on its wings and fuselage were plainly visible. Our section continued on course until the Japanese aircraft was at a "five o'clock low" position, and then we made a 180-degree descending turn to the right, straightening out into a shallow power dive but rapidly closing the distance on the target – my No 2 provided top-cover.

'At maybe 30 yards I opened and held fire. Tracer hits were seen on the wing roots of what appeared to be an Army 97, whose pilot immediately pulled into a sharp left-hand climbing turn. I pulled my Mohawk into a right hand climbing turn, and in the process of completing a 360-degree turn, the enemy was seen to be going down in an increasingly steep dive, with black smoke pouring back from the engine. Then a parachute streamed back from the cockpit. After I saw the aircraft hit the ground and the parachute descending toward the jungle, we turned onto a northerly course for Tezpur.'

Although Garnett had thought that his opponent was a Nakajima Ki-27 'Nate' fighter, it was in fact a similar looking Tachikawa Ki-36 'Ida' army cooperation aircraft of the 89th Sentai, flown by Capt Nagasawa.

That same day recently reformed No 155 Sqn, based at St Thomas Mount, near Madras, received its first Mohawks, with a further batch delivered a week later. The unit was commanded by 12-victory ace Sqn Ldr Donald 'Dimsie' Stones, who recalled his frustrations at getting

This poor quality, but interesting, photograph shows AR677/OQ-D of No 5 Sqn on the wing in June 1942 during the unit's spell in northern Assam conducting operations over northern Burma. The shot was taken from a Dakota of No 31 Sqn that was performing a re-supply mission to the isolated outpost at Fort Hertz. AR677 later served with No 155 Sqn, and claimed the type's final aerial victory with the RAF on 9 November 1943 (*via G R Pitchfork*)

Flt Lt Keith MacEwan surveys the bullet ridden rear fuselage of his Mohawk at Dinjan after an attack on Myitkyina on 8 July 1942. It was whilst flying this aircraft on 6 April that MacEwan 'blooded' the Mohawk in RAF service when he attacked, and damaged, an E8N2 'Dave' floatplane from the IJN cruiser *Kumano* over the Bay of Bengal (*A K MacEwan*)

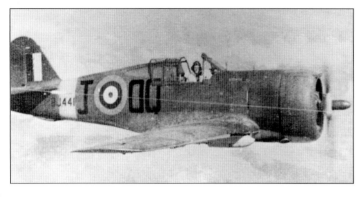

Mohawk IV BJ441/OQ-J of No 5 Sqn patrols over the Brahmaputra River from Agartala in October 1942 when the unit provided the defence of the port city of Calcutta. It is wearing the standard dark green/dark earth/sky colours of the period, although the code letters are black rather than the more usual 'sky' colour. BJ441 is being flown by Sgt Derek Wicks, who, on 12 February 1943, shot down a Ki-43 'Oscar' that duly became No 5 Sqn's final victory with the Mohawk (*D Wicks*)

Flt Sgt Rod Lawrence of No 5 Sqn climbs out of his Mohawk IV BB925/OQ-R that he had decorated with a large red maple leaf and the head of a timber wolf to proclaim him as a Canadian! It also wears the names *ROD and LOIS* beneath the cockpit. He was flying BB925 on 7 October 1942 when he destroyed a Ki-48 'Lily' bomber over Akyab and shared in the probable destruction of a Ki-21 'Sally' the following January. These claims made Lawrence the second most successful Commonwealth pilot on the Mohawk (*R R Lawrence*)

his unit ready for combat in his autobiography;

'My target date for the unit's operational status had receded due to all our maintenance problems, but I was able to report that we should be operational by the end of September, or early October.'

THE ARAKAN

On 2 October No 5 Sqn returned south to Agartala, in Bengal, so that it could conduct bomber escort missions and fighter patrols over the Arakan peninsula in support of a limited Allied offensive. On the 7th, Sqn Ldr Pitt-Brown led ten Mohawks on an escort to Akyab. En route they spotted four Kawasaki Ki-48 'Lily' bombers, and having first reported them, Canadian Flt Sgt Rod Lawrence left his formation and attacked the aircraft, as he later described;

'I did not realise until I was almost ready to attack that I was all alone. This particular bomber had only one rear gunner, with a single machine gun, and as I had six, and was making a straight astern attack, he was no big deal. As I kept firing in a continuous burst, I saw the rear gunner disappear. I continued firing to within 35 yards, by which point the bomber's undercarriage was hanging down and its right engine was on fire. I pulled out of the attack and watched the bomber ditch in the water.'

He also noted in his logbook, 'Strip torn off and congratulations at same time! Broke formation – was a bad boy'.

Soon afterwards No 155 Sqn moved to Alipore in the suburbs of Calcutta, and on the morning of the 30th it flew its first offensive sortie, as Sqn Ldr Stones noted;

'I was to take our 13 serviceable Mohawks up to Imphal for a ground strafing attack on the Japanese-occupied airfield at Shwebo, in Burma, 200 miles southeast of Imphal, on the banks of the Irrawaddy River.'

The unit headed out across the misty jungle-clad mountains of Manipur province, as Stones recalled;

'As we descended, we could see a wide plain below us, beyond which lay our target. I caught sight of Shwebo township and took the squadron straight down towards the airfield, which I could now see ahead. It was deserted, apart from one twin-engined transport aircraft in the parking area. Plt Off Meyer, wide to port of me, destroyed this with an accurate burst.'

The rest of the formation then attacked various airfield facilities, causing significant damage. However, on his return to base Stones was ordered to Madras, where an Army provost officer, with whom he had previously clashed, had

started court martial proceedings against him. In the event he was severely reprimanded, and had to revert to the rank of flight lieutenant for using bad language in his dealings with the provost officer, or, as the veteran Stones later referred to him, 'that jumped-up policeman!' Either way, No 155 Sqn lost an experienced CO, Stones being replaced soon afterwards by ex-Malta ace Sqn Ldr C G St D 'Porky' Jeffries.

Soon afterwards, No 155 Sqn joined up with No 5 Sqn in No 169 Wing, which had been formed on 3 October 1942 with Pitt-Brown as Wing Leader and seven-victory ace Wg Cdr Jimmy Elsdon as CO. Ground attacks and escorts then ensued, and further aerial action came on 10 November. That morning, eight Mohawks from No 155 Sqn had escorted six Blenheim IVs and Bisleys from Nos 113 and 60 Sqns in a low-level bombing attack on Akyab docks. At around 1100 hrs over the target, the force encountered Ki-43 'Oscar' fighters of the JAAF's elite 64th Sentai, led by Capt Haruyasu Maruo, who were themselves on an escort mission.

The 'Oscars' destroyed a Blenheim and two escorting Mohawks, with a third Mohawk having part of its rudder shot away and its pilot forced to land at Chittagong. However, on the credit side Plt Off T Buddle shot down an 'Oscar' in a tight turning fight when it suddenly made a right hand elliptical turn and fired, but missed, giving the Mohawk pilot a close range shot which blew off part of the Ki-43's mainplane and sent it crashing into the sea.

A second 'Oscar' was shared between Flt Lt Peter Rathie and a gunner in one of the Blenhiems, while a third Ki-43 was also credited to Australian Plt Off Alan Haley, who had gained three victories and a damaged over Malta the previous year. There is some doubt about this claim, however, although if valid, it was his fifth, and final, success, for on 1 January he was shot down and killed by anti-aircraft fire over the Chindwin. These were the squadron's first victories.

Later that day nine Blenheims (from Nos 60, 113 and 34 Sqns) mounted a further attack on Akyab, and this time the escort was provided by No 5 Sqn's Mohawks, led by Wing Leader Sqn Ldr Pitt-Brown. They too met Ki-43s from the 64th Sentai, as Bill Pitt-Brown recalled;

'I was on the left wing of the high escort, and as the harbour of Akyab became visible ahead, I made a call of "Bandits '12 o'clock high'". Simultaneously, I saw two tracers pass diagonally across my windscreen and automatically broke left in a steep climbing turn. Somehow, shortly afterwards, I found myself in a right hand turn at approximately a "two o'clock" position. Tightening the turn, with a large deflection I fired a long burst. During this time a long stream of white vapour appeared from the fuselage of the "Type 01".

'After continuing the right hand circle I finished up behind the "Oscar", which was venting fuel, but at a range of 25-30 yards, where-upon the "Type 01" did a half roll and dived away steeply. Looking around, the sky was empty, so I

No 155 Sqn's first CO was Sqn Ldr 'Dimsie' Stones, who had 'made ace' during the fighting over France, Britain and Malta. Having brought his unit to an operational state, he only led it on its first mission before being removed after an altercation with a Provost Officer in Madras! (*D Winton via J Linn*)

When Sqn Ldr Stones led his unit on its first operation (a strafing attack on the airfield at Shwebo) on 30 October 1942, he was flying BJ442/Y. The fighter survived with the unit until September 1943 – appreciably longer than Stones had managed! (*author's collection*)

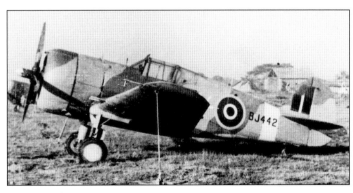

In November 1942 No 169 Wing was formed, with Sqn Ldr William 'Bill' Pitt-Brown as Wing Leader. He successfully led the wing in this aircraft, BS790, and on 10 November 1942 he shot down a Ki-43 'Oscar' during the largest combat ever fought between Mohawks and the JAAF. As a Wing Leader, Pitt-Brown was able to adorn his fighter with his initials (*W H Pitt-Brown*)

changed course and headed back up the Arakan coast to Feni.'

Although Pitt-Brown had made his call prior to attacking the Ki-43s, unbeknownst to him, his radio was unserviceable, so nobody heard his warning. However, the CO's action was witnessed by Flt Sgt Rod Lawrence, who recalled 'I saw Wing Leader Pitt-Brown shoot one down, and I also saw two Blenheims go down'. This was Pitt-Brown's only air combat success.

A confused dogfight then ensued, during which Sgt F A Gore made a quarter attack on a Ki-43 and scored hits all over its forward fuselage, causing the canopy to shatter. The fighter fell away trailing smoke, but it could only be claimed as a probable. Meanwhile, Flt Lt Joe Cunliffe drove off other 'Oscars' that were attacking a Blenheim, damaging two. Plt Off D F Bullen damaged two more after he too came to the Blenheim's aid, and yet another Ki-43 was damaged by Plt Off John Lee. The latter was then attacked by other fighters, and with his Mohawk damaged, he was forced to head for home.

Plt Off R S Tovey, meanwhile, engaged another 'Oscar' that began to trail white vapour. He then collided with his intended victim, and as Tovey headed for home, Sgt Maj Ito was killed when his shattered 'Oscar' crashed into the sea.

It had been a successful engagement for No 5 Sqn, and the Mohawk Wing as a whole. Interestingly, after this first major combat, the pilots had discovered that their little Mohawks could actually outturn the highly manoeuvrable 'Oscars', as Sgt Stuart Garnett observed;

'The manoeuvrability was good, and it was found that if the speed was kept up – 180 to 200 mph – the aircraft could turn well with the "Type 01 Oscars". A high-speed stall was practically unknown.'

Two weeks later, No 155 Sqn moved to Agartala to operate alongside No 5 Sqn, and on 1 December both units flew together as a wing in a formation practice for the first time. On the 5th, 'A' Flight of No 155 Sqn detached to Chittagong, and that afternoon the unit scrambled to intercept an incoming bombing raid that boasted a fighter escort. The Mohawks were vectored in from ahead and below, and they were soon involved in a general melee. Flt Lt Peter Rathie, who was to become the most successful RAF Mohawk pilot, wrote in his combat report;

'The "Type 01" had its belly towards me, and it was going down. I dived after him. He turned and saw me and went into a left hand turn. He turned three times to the left and I turned inside him, giving him several squirts. He then climbed straight and I climbed, gaining on him, and I gave him another squirt. He did a sort of spin stall, so I waited above until he came out of it and then I dived on him, giving him another squirt. I was able to keep him in range, so I continued firing. I closed to 30 yards and gave him the rest of my ammunition in one long burst.'

Rathie had shot down Capt Masuzo Otani of the 64th Sentai, and he also damaged a second 'Oscar', as had Plt Off Peter MacDonald.

The limited offensive down the Arakan peninsula had Maungdaw and Buithidaung as the initial objectives, although the topography facing the Allied troops was always going to pose as much of a challenge as the enemy. Further fighter sweeps continued, and on 10 December six-kill Singapore ace Sgt Henry Nicholls and Flt Sgt Freeman flew a 'Rhubarb', leaving Imphal at 1250 hrs to attack river and rail communications. The next day Rathie led Nicholls and two others on an escort mission in support of four Hurricanes sent to attack Akyab – No 5 Sqn also sortied a number of Mohawks.

The latter unit claimed another aerial success during the afternoon of 21 December when, during a sweep to Akyab in clear and sunny weather, Flg Off P M Bellinger shot down a Mitsubishi Ki-21 'Sally' bomber.

The Arakan offensive led to a marked increase in Japanese air activity, whilst the RAF continued to mount attacks on various targets, including Akyab.

On 19 January 1943, No 5 Sqn escorted Blenheims from No 113 Sqn on another raid that was intercepted by eight Ki-43s. Six of the Mohawks peeled off to engage, and Flg Off A S 'Smokey' Boyes, who hailed from Argentina, damaged one and then turned on another, which collided with him and crashed into the sea. Boyes returned safely minus some four feet of wingtip. Joe Cunliffe claimed a probable on what was a red letter day for him, as he was also notified that he was to be awarded a DFC.

In order to be closer to the action, No 5 Sqn detached down the coast to a beach strip code named 'Hove', which was the closest advanced strip to Akyab, in preparation for a large operation planned for 22 January. At dawn, squadrons from No 224 Group began a large-scale operation aimed at disrupting enemy supply routes. Although there was little sign of the JAAF, No 5 Sqn did claim a Ki-21 of the 98th Sentai as probably destroyed.

No 155 Sqn had also been active early in the New Year, and it continued to build up its operational tempo by flying bomber escort missions, often in bad weather.

During the last week of the month, in spite of much RAF activity over the Arakan, there was little sign of the JAAF. Indeed, Allied intelligence in-theatre worked out that Japanese fighter and bomber units would usually conduct numerous operations over several days and then withdraw, before suddenly reappearing in strength a week or two later.

The only time the RAF encountered the JAAF during the final week of January came during the morning of the 28th, when 22 Mohawk pilots led by Bill Pitt-Brown combined in a sweep to Akyab, as the wing records stated;

'The wing flew in stepped up fours at between 8000 ft and 16,000 ft west-to-east across Akyab and returned across the north of the island. A report of "Bandits 'seven o'clock'" was given over the R/T and some pilots reported seeing Hurricanes. Sqn Ldr Jeffries, flying at 14,000 ft, reported a single-seat thin-tailed Japanese aircraft diving at high speed, and apparently smoking, through his formation. He was able to give it one good burst at approximately 70 yards range using full deflection. The enemy aircraft continued diving towards Akyab Island and is claimed destroyed. This was later confirmed when group reported a Jap pilot as having been seen to bale out at the time Sqn Ldr Jeffries opened fire.'

Another ace who served with No 155 Sqn was Cornishman Sgt Henry Nicholls, who had claimed six victories flying Hurricanes with No 232 Sqn over Malaya and Sumatra in January-February 1942, prior to being evacuated to India (*via C H Thomas*)

Flt Lt C S Courtney-Clarke of No 5 Sqn later recalled the incident. 'I saw "Clipper Leader" get one Jap, otherwise it was a "stooge" trip'. This was Sqn Ldr 'Porky' Jeffries' only success while flying the Mohawk, and it gave him the unique distinction of being the sole Commonwealth ace to make an air-to-air claim in the Curtiss fighter.

The following day, No 155 Sqn moved north to Imphal to provide ground strafing support for Maj Gen Orde Wingate's Chindit expedition. No 5 Sqn, now led by Sqn Ldr Guy Hogan, remained in the south, where it continued operations in spite of the lack of Allied success in the Arakan offensive.

The only Commonwealth ace to score an air-to-air kill in the Mohawk was Sqn Ldr 'Porky' Jeffries of No 155 Sqn, whose sole success against the Japanese was a Ki-43 that he initially claimed as a probable, but which was later upgraded to a victory (*author's collection*)

Following a photo-reconnaissance escort for several Hurricanes on 12 February, No 5 Sqn claimed its final confirmed Mohawk victory. Two fighters had landed at Maungdaw to refuel after completing their mission, only to be scrambled, as Sgt Derek Wicks recalled;

'We were jumped by four "Type 01s" right over the airfield. "Stu" (Stuart Garnett) and I had a wizard series of dogfights. I took plenty of hits on my kite – 'D' – totalling two in the armour plating, four in the petrol tank and many in the wings and the prop. I did get several good squirts at an 01, which went in – confirmed by witnesses on the 'drome – and another damaged. The others were chased off. The whole thing took place well below 3000 ft. My kill was confirmed in writing by Sqn Ldr Hogan, OC No 5 Sqn.'

Derek Wicks' victim was none other than Maj Yasumi Yagi, CO of the 64th Sentai, who had been killed by a single round to the head. His fighter crashed west of Rathedaung.

From mid-March, it was the turn of the Japanese to mount an air offensive resulting in many air combats, although most of the action came the way of the Hurricane units. However, on the 29th No 5 Sqn's

Sqn Ldr Jeffries' assigned aircraft in early 1943 was BB928/Z, which wore his personal nose art – a fire breathing Welsh dragon above the inscription *Cymru am Byth*. However, what makes this aircraft unique is that it is the only Mohawk known to have carried a scoreboard that included Jeffries' claims against the Luftwaffe, the Regia Aeronautica and the JAAF (*Paul Sortehaug via B Cull*)

Mohawks engaged a dozen Ki-43s late in the afternoon as they performed a fighter sweep ahead of bombers sent to hit forward Allied positions. At 1520 hrs, Flt Lt Jonathan Rashleigh led six Mohawks off from 'Reindeer' strip as the 'Oscars' flew over Maungdaw, and soon a whirling dogfight ensued. Flt Lt Rashleigh claimed a probable, while Plt Off John Lee attacked another fighter from astern and sent it down trailing smoke – he too was credited with a probable victory.

Although he was not credited with a confirmed victory, Flg Off John Lee was one of only two RAF pilots to make five claims with the Mohawk. Awarded a DFC, he was later killed whilst flying Hurricanes (*via J Linn*)

Flg Off John Lee's Mohawk wore this impressive personal marking on the nose (*A K MacEwan via J Linn*)

Flg Off John Lee, in BJ439/V, leads 'B' Flight, No 5 Sqn, down the Arakan coast in early 1943. This was his regular aircraft, and he was flying it on 29 March when he claimed an 'Oscar' probable and damaged two more. Lee also flew it on No 5 Sqn's final Mohawk mission on 30 May (*G J C Hogan*)

Lee was then attacked and had several further combats, claiming two more Ki-43s damaged to become one of only two RAF pilots to make five claims with the Mohawk. His return was described by a colleague;

'A little while later in came John Lee with nothing more than a scratch on his shoulder, but with his aircraft so riddled with bullet holes that it was virtually a write off.'

The JAAF was back in strength the next day too, hitting 'Hay' and 'Lyons' strips. Among those aircraft scrambled by No 5 Sqn in response was a section of four Mohawks from 'Reindeer', led by Sqn Ldr Guy Hogan. Over Maungdaw at 15,000 ft, Hogan spotted 'Oscars' some 3000 ft below him and led his section into attack the enemy fighters out of the sun. The Mohawk pilots claimed two probables and a damaged. Guy Hogan remembered;

'It is difficult to recount a dogfight, as it all happens so quickly – one second it's all action, the next there is not another aircraft in sight. However, I think it probable that Flg Off Paddy Chancellor did attack my "Type 01", as he would have followed me into the initial attack. After I took evasive action from another "01", I did not see any of our aircraft – only an "01" out of the corner of my eye, emitting smoke. Chancellor was killed less than a month later.'

These were No 5 Sqn's final air combat claims.

Enemy raids continued, and on 5 April, with No 5 Sqn away, a raid was reported approaching Agartala, as the wing records noted. 'One Mohawk piloted by Wg Cdr Elsdon was our only defence. Actually, the raid was a number of B-25s returning here to refuel'. However, the following day another raid was reported approaching at 1400 hrs. This time it was the enemy, and 18 Ki-21s without escort attacked Agartala, causing considerable damage – the frustrated Jimmy Elsdon was unable to get airborne in the sole Mohawk on the airfield.

The situation for the British continued to deteriorate on the ground, and by mid April the 14th Division had retreated to positions surrounding Maungdaw. There was, however, only sporadic JAAF activity over the front during this period. No 5 Sqn flew its final Mohawk operation on 20 May, and by early July it had re-equipped with Hurricane IIDs.

IMPHAL

Having moved up to Imphal, in northeastern India, in February 1943, No 155 Sqn found that the approaching monsoon created additional difficulties, and its first encounter with enemy aircraft in this area did not take place until 20

April. During the afternoon, ten Mohawks scrambled when 20 enemy aircraft were detected approaching from the south. Only the sections led by Flt Lt Peter Rathie and Flg Off McGregor succeeded in making contact with the enemy, however.

Targeting a formation of Ki-21s, Rathie managed to damage one of the bombers and McGregor made several attacks on another. He saw smoke pour from its engines, allowing him to claiming it as a probable. Escorting 'Oscars' then intervened, and Rathie's section engaged the fighters as they went after McGregor and his wingman. A series of vicious dogfights ensued, with Rathie hitting a Ki-43 with a long burst of fire in the engine and cockpit, which he duly claimed as a probable, and McGregor made a similar claim after a diving attack on an 'Oscar' which spun in from about 3000 ft. Eventually, both Rathie and McGregor managed to disengage and escape, although their wingmen were posted as missing.

The following morning, No 155 Sqn had another unequal battle against an incoming raid on Imphal, during which Flg Off Tim Meyer, who hailed from Trinidad and is remembered as being a superb pilot, hit an 'Oscar' in the wings and claimed it as damaged. This proved to be No 155 Sqn's last combat with the JAAF for some months.

The squadron returned to Agartala in June, from where numerous bombing and strafing sorties were conducted. The mission generated on 19 August was typical of those flown during this period, Sqn Ldr Jeffries leading five Mohawks to the Mawlaik area in heavy cloud. Diving attacks were made from 1500 ft, with at least 14 direct hits being recorded on enemy buildings. A number of sampans seen moored on the banks of the Chindwin River were also strafed, and several were sunk, although one of the 20-lb bombs on Jeffries' Mohawk hung up.

The unit returned to Imphal on 10 September, and on the 24th Jeffries led 11 aircraft up the Chindwin River on a ground-strafing sweep. A subsequent intelligence report generated following this mission indicated that 50+ enemy troops had been killed by the Mohawk attacks.

On 9 October Jeffries flew as a pathfinder for an attack by Hurricanes of No 258 Sqn on Webula, and later in the day he led a strafing mission

These Mohawks of No 155 Sqn (BS798/B, BT470/F and AR661/V) patrol near Agartala in August 1943 – shortly before the unit moved north to Imphal. They wear the interim yellow-outlined blue/white roundels, with yellow wingtips for recognition. The nearest aircraft, BS798/B, was flown by Flg Off Harry Bishop on 9 November 1943, when the Mohawk fought with the JAAF in the air for the final time (*H Bishop*)

During his final few weeks with No 155 Sqn, Sqn Ldr Jeffries regularly flew BJ545/C, including on the final sortie of his long tour on 2 November 1943. One week later, during the Mohawks' final aerial battle, it was flown by Sgt McCormack (*H Bishop*)

On 9 November 1943, Flg Off Tony Dunford, in AR677/V, was scrambled from Imphal against an incoming raid and attacked one of the escorting fighters, which he shot down into the jungle to claim the RAF's final victory with the Mohawk (*via D Linn*)

against Japanese positions along a ridge. Forty-eight hours later, he led another strike on Japanese troops, and this was repeated the following day. Ground attack missions continued for the next few weeks, and this pattern of operations was only broken on 9 November when, for the first time in seven months, No 155 Sqn came across the JAAF in the air. That morning, two Mohawks had tried to intercept a high-flying Mitsubishi Ki-46 'Dinah' reconnaissance aircraft, and a second scramble several hours later also proved to be abortive.

These flights were the precursors to a raid, and at noon 16 Ki-21 bombers, with an escort of 'Oscars', attacked the Imphal strip. Four Mohawks scrambled and attempted to cut off the homeward bound bombers. Flg Off Tony Dunford, who was flying AR677/V, recorded in his diary;

'A memorable day started off with Plt Offs Tommy Buddle and Bruce Pinch getting within half a mile of a Japanese reconnaissance aeroplane and recognising it. They could not fire as the Nip stuck his nose down and screamed off home. At about 1130 hrs, all kites were scrambled when 17 bombers and six fighters attacked the strip, destroying a few aircraft on the ground, killing a few types and injuring others. I was up with Mac Edwards as my No 2. Sighted an "Oscar" on Bishop's tail and engaged the Jap for about three minutes, using all my ammunition. Saw plenty of strikes on his wings, and he turned onto his back and screamed down. Bishop saw it hit the ground and burst into flames. I claimed the "Oscar" as one destroyed.'

Dunford's victim – the last to fall to a Mohawk whilst in British colours – was probably Cpl Kitaoka of the 50th Sentai, who crashed to the northeast of Palel, where the wreckage of his fighter was later found. On 13 November 'Porky' Jeffries handed over command of No 155 Sqn to Sqn Ldr Denis Winton, the squadron diary noting that it had been Jeffries' fourth operational tour, and that 'his great experience, keenness and qualities of leadership did much to raise the efficiency of the squadron to a high standard'. Winton described his ace predecessor thus;

'Short and stocky, with fair hair, a round face, blue eyes and a permanent sort of crooked, twisted smile as though he was waiting to tell a funny story. I am not surprised that he was never shot down, I don't think the enemy had an opportunity to see him. He was a great character, and a marvellous chap.'

No 155 Sqn continued on operations with its weary Mohawks until 6 January 1944, when the unit flew its little Curtiss fighters to Kanchrapara for disposal and duly re-equipped with Spitfire VIIIs.

Although only seeing service in small numbers, the Mohawk was a valuable addition to the RAF's modest strength in India during 1942-43, and the fighter is remembered with affection by those who flew it. Indeed, the aircraft was one of the few Allied types that could actually turn with nimble JAAF fighters such as the Ki-27 and Ki-43.

APPENDICES

French Pilots with at least five Hawk 75 victories

Name	Unit	Hawk 75 Claims (destroyed and probable)	Total Claims	Area	Remarks
E Marin-la-Meslée	I/5	16 + 4		F	
C Plubeau	II/4	14 + 4		F	WIA 9/6/40
M Dorance	I/5	14 + 3	14 + 4	F	
J-M Accart	I/5	12 + 4		F	WIA 1/6/40
A Vasatko (Czech)	I/5	12 + 2	14 + 4	F	
G Lefol	II/5 and I/5	12 + 1		F	
F Perina (Czech)	I/5	11 + 2	12 + 2	F	WIA 3/6/40
M Tallent	I/5	11 + 1		F	
L Vuillemain	I/5	10 + 4	11 + 4	F/A	
F Morel	I/5	10 + 3		F	KIA 18/5/40
M Rouquette	I/5	9 + 6	10 + 6	F/A	
G Baptizet	II/4	9 + 4		F	
D Penzini	I/5	9 + 2		F	
A Legrand	II/5	9 + 1		F/A	
J-M Rey	I/5	9 + 0		F	WIA 18/5/40
J Bressieux	I/5	9 + 0		F/A	
F Warnier	I/5	8 + 2		F	
M Parnière	I/5	8 + 1		F	WIA 3/6/40
R Huvet	II/5	8 + 0		F/A	KIA 8/11/42
G Tesseraud	II/4	7 + 4	8 + 4	F	WIA 9/11/42
J Paulhan	II/4	7 + 3		F	WIA 9/6/40
H Monraisse	II/5	7 + 2		F/A	
E Salès	II/5	7 + 2		F	
E Guillaume	I/4	7 + 1		F	
A de la Chapelle	II/4	7 + 1		F	
A Casenobe	II/4	7 + 0		F	
R Guieu	II/4	7 + 0		F	KIA 7/6/40
J Girou	I/5	7 + 0		F	
T Vybiral (Czech)	I/5	7 + 0		F	
G Muselli	I/5	6 + 4		F	
P Villacèque	II/5	6 + 2		F/A	WIA 8/11/42
J Joire	I/4	6 + 0		F	WIA 25/5/40
J Klan (Czech)	II/5	5 + 2		F	
P Villey	II/4	5 + 1		F	KIA 25/5/40
A Bouhy	II/5	5 + 1		F/A	KIA 8/11/42
J Hotellier	I/4	5 + 0		F	WIA and PoW 26/5/40
H Boitelet	I/5	5 + 0		F	
M Hébrard	II/5	5 + 0	7 + 0	F	
A Petitjean-Roget	II/5	5 + 0		F	

French Aces with at least one Hawk 75 victory

L Svetlik (Czech)	II/5	4 + 2	5 + 2	F	
R Rubin	II/4	4 + 2	5 + 2	F	
G Lemare	I/4	3 + 1	12 + 1	F/A	
A Moret	III/2	3 + 0	8 + 0	F	
J Cucumel	I/4	3 + 0	9 + 1	F	
R Puda (Czech)	II/4	3 + 0	5 + 0	F	
L Delfino	I/4	2 + 2	16 + 4	F/A	
E Corniglion-Molinier	III/2	2 + 1	6 + 3	F	
M Le Blanc	III/2	2 + 1	5 + 1	F	KIA 9/11/42
J Kremski (Pole)	DAT Bourges	2 + 0	9 + 1	F	
G Tricaud	II/5	2 + 0	5 + 1	A	KIA 8/11/42
G Pissotte	III/2	1 + 1	8 + 1	F	
G Elmlinger	III/2	1 + 0	7 + 1	F	WIA 9/6/40
B Kosinski (Pole)	DAT Bourges	1 + 0	5 + 2	F	
M Haegelen	DAT Bourges	1 + 0	23 + 2	F	
M Romey	III/2	0 + 1	5 + 4	F	KIA 13/6/40

Note

In the l'Armée de l'Air, when a pilot shared in the destruction of an enemy aircraft with a squadronmate, he was credited with a full victory, not a fraction, although his unit was awarded only a single victory

Key

F – France
A – Africa
KIA – Killed In Action
WIA – Wounded In Action
PoW – Prisoner of War

USAAC Aces and notable non-ace P-36 Pilots

Name	Unit	P-36 Claims	Total Claims	Area
H M Brown	47th PS	2/-/-	7/-/1	P
F S Gabreski	45th PS	-	34.5/1/5	P
W F Haney	45th PS	-	5/3/3	P
M Moore	46th PS	-/-/1	-/-/1	P
J C Price	50th PS	-	5/-/1	C
P M Rasmussen	46th PS	1/-/-	2/-/-	P
R H Rogers	47th PS	-/1/-	1/1/-	P
L M Sanders	46th PS	1/-/-	1/-/-	P
G H Sterling	45th PS	1/-/-	1/-/-	P
G S Welch	47th PS	-	16/1/-	P
H Zemke	36th PS	-	17+2sh/2/9	US

Key

P – Pacific and Alaska
C – Panama Canal Zone
US – Continental USA

Finnish Hawk 75 Aces

Name	Rank	Unit	Hawk 75 Score	Total Score	Notes
K Tervo	1Lt	2/LeLv 32	14.25	21.25	(KIA 20/8/43)
K Karhila	2Lt	1/LeLv 32	12.25	32.25	
E Koskinen	WO	2/LeLv 32	10.333	11.333	(ACC 11/1/45)
Y Pallasvuo	2Lt	2/LeLv 32	9	13	(KIA 3/7/44)
J Hillo	1Lt	1/LeLv 32	8.333	8.333	
V Virtanen	SSgt	2/LeLv 32	8	8	
A Bremer	Capt	2/LeLv 32	7.5	7.5	
N Erkinheimo	SSgt	1/LeLv 32	6.75	10.75	(KIFA 16/11/43)
A Gerdt	SSgt	3/LeLv 32	6	6	
A Kiljunen	SSgt	1/LeLv 32	6	6	
K Lahtela	Capt	1/LeLv 32	5.75	10.75	
P Berg	Capt	1/LeLv 32	5.5	10.5	KIA 1/11/41
P Nurminen	Capt	3/LeLv 32	5.5	5.5	(PoW 19/3/43)
P Salminen	MSgt	2/LeLv 32	5.5	6	
S Alapuro	1Lt	3/LeLv 32	5	5	

Finnish Aces with some Hawk 75 victories

Name	Rank	Unit	Hawk 75 Score	Total Score	Notes
M Kirjonen	2Lt	1/LeLv 32	4.25	9.75	
L Jutila	SSgt	3/LeLv 32	4	7.5	(KIA 17/6/43)
V Evinen	Capt	3/LeLv 32	2.5	6	(KIA 25/6/44)
O Ehrnrooth	Maj	E/LeLv 32	2	5	(KIFA 27/3/43)
M Fräntilä	MSgt	3/LeLv 32	1.5	5.5	

Note

The rank stated is the highest achieved by the pilot whilst flying the Hawk 75 except for Kullervo Lahtela, who returned to command the squadron as a major, but did not make any further claims.

Key (note entry in parenthesis indicates that the event occurred in another unit)
KIA – Killed In Action
ACC – Accident (killed)
KIFA – Killed In Flying Accident
PoW – Prisoner of War

Commonwealth Aces that flew the Mohawk

Name	Service	Unit	Mohawk Claims	Total Claims	Area
A C Bosman	SAAF	4 SAAF	-	8+3sh/1/3	EA
Count M Czernin	RAF	146	-	13+5sh/3.5/3+2sh	Ind
A Duncan	SAAF	5 SAAF	-	4?/1/-	SA
T A F Elsdon	RAF	169 Wg	-	7/-/2	Ind
J E Frost	SAAF	5 SAAF	-	4+2sh/2+2sh/2.5	SA
D W Golding	SAAF	4 SAAF	-	8+3sh/2/2	SA
S Heglund	Nor	FTL	-	15+1sh/6/6+1sh	NA
J D W Human	SAAF	5 SAAF	-	5/-/0.5	SA
C G StD Jeffries	RAF	155	1/-/-	4+2sh/2/2	Ind
D V D Lacey	SAAF	6 SAAF	-	5/2/5	SA
D H Loftus	SAAF	7 SAAF	-	4+1sh/-/3	SA
H T Nicholls	RAF	155	-	6/1/3	Ind
M S Osler	SAAF	6 SAAF	-	9.5/-/2	SA
R Pare	SAAF	5 SAAF	-	6/-/0.5	SA
J E Parsonson	SAAF	3 SAAF	-/-/- + 1 on ground	4.5/-/3 + 1 on ground	EA
H M Stephen	RAF	AHQ	-	9+8sh/3/7	Ind
D W A Stones	RAF	155	-	7+5sh/4.5/4+2sh	Ind
C A van Vliet*	SAAF	10 SAAF	-	4/-/1	SA
L A Wilmot	SAAF	6 SAAF	-	4.5/-/-	SA

Notable non-Ace Commonwealth Mohawk Pilots

Name	Service	Unit	Mohawk Claims	Total Claims	Area
C V Bargh	RNZAF	5	-	3/2/-	Ind
A H Haley	RAAF	155	1/-/	4/-/1	Ind
W J N Lee	RAF	5	-/1/4	-/1/4	Ind
W Pitt-Brown	RAF	5, 169 Wg	1/-/-	1/-/-	Ind
P Rathie	RAF	155	1.5/1/2	1+2sh/1/3	Ind
H E N Wildsmith	SAAF	4 SAAF	-	4/1/1	EA

Key
Ind – India and Burma
EA – East Africa
SA – South Africa
NA – North America
* – van Vliet has less than five victories but is shown because of his inclusion in *Aces High*, as there is doubt as to his actual score

P-36A Hawk

Hawk 75A-1

Hawk 75A-2

Hawk 75A-4

Hawk 75A-6

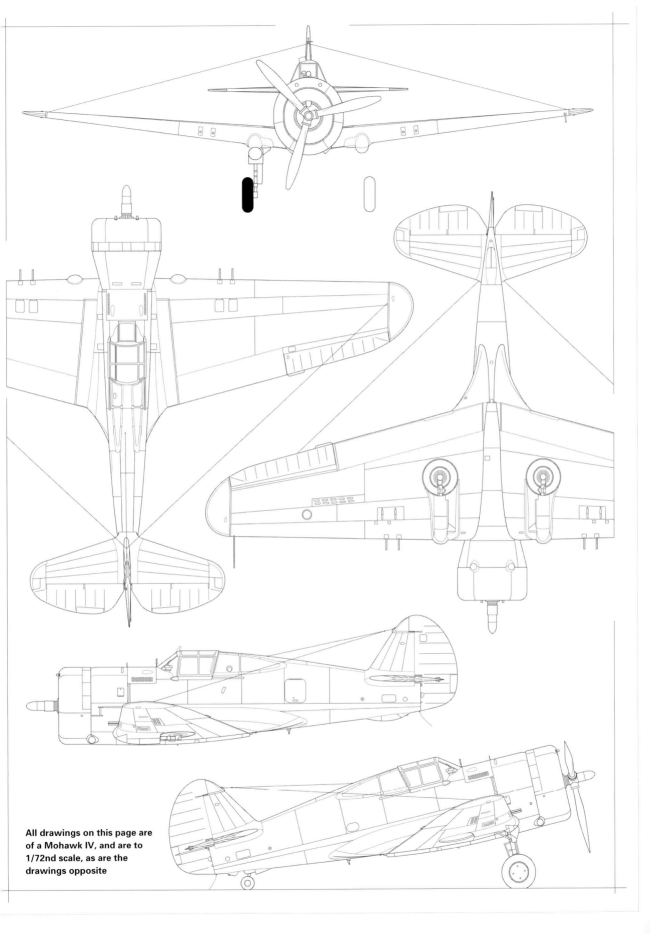

All drawings on this page are
of a Mohawk IV, and are to
1/72nd scale, as are the
drawings opposite

COLOUR PLATES

1

Hawk 75A-1 N°7 (X806) of GC I/5's 1st *escadrille*, Reims, spring 1939

The first Hawk 75s reached France in late February 1939 and were issued to GC I/5's 1st *escadrille*. Its pilots would duly develop all the combat tactics employed by the *l'Armée de l'Air* from September 1939, and this is perhaps why GC 1/5 obtained the most victories with the Hawk 75 in 1940. N°7 was flown for the first time by future ten-kill ace Sgt François Morel on 28 February 1939. Remaining in natural metal until camouflaged in the summer of 1939, the aircraft served with GC I/5 throughout the Phoney War, but was damaged in a forced-landing after being shot up whilst engaging an He 111P of II./KG 55 on 18 May 1940. The Heinkel crashed near Branges, and the Hawk 75's pilot, Sgt Gérard Muselli (six victories), received a share in the credit for its destruction.

2

Hawk 75A-2 N°151 (U051) '1' of GC I/5's 1st *escadrille*, flown by Cne Jean-Mary Accart, Suippes and St-Dizier, May 1940

Of all the Curtiss fighters flown by the *l'Armée de l'Air* in the Battle of Francem, Hawk 75A-2 N°151 (U051) was almost certainly the most successful in terms of aerial kills. From October 1939, it was personal mount of GC 1/5's CO, Cne Jean-Mary Accart, who achieved all 12 of his confirmed victories in it between 10 May and 1 June 1940. The fighter was lost on the latter date, however, when it was struck by return fire from He 111Hs of 9./KG 53. Badly wounded, Accart was forced to bale out over Frasne. N°151 had also been used by ranking Hawk 75 ace Lt Edmond Marin-la-Meslée to claim a kill on 19 May 1940, thus taking its overall tally to 13.

3

Hawk 75A-2 N°158 (U058) '2' of GC I/5's 1st *escadrille*, flown by Lt Edmond Marin-la-Meslée, Suippes and St-Dizier, May 1940

Hawk 75A-2 N°158 (U058) was the personal mount of Lt Edmond Marin-la-Meslée from October 1939. He achieved a number of his early successes in the aircraft until it was written off in a forced landing on 18 May 1940. Like Sgt Gérard Muselli's N°7, N°158 was hit by return fire from an He 111P of II./KG 55 that caused its cockpit to fill with petrol fumes. Although badly affected by the latter, Marin-la-Meslée managed to belly land N°158 at St Dizier. He received new Hawk 75A-3 N°217 as a replacement, and flew it until 1942.

4

Hawk 75A-1 N°14 (X813) '7' of GC I/5's 2nd *escadrille*, flown by Sgt Chef Jérémie Bressieux, Suippes and St-Dizier, May 1940

GC I/5's 2nd *escadrille* also achieved many victories during the Battle of France, and could boast nine aces by the time the Franco-German Armistice came into effect on 25 June 1940. Sgt Chef Jérémie Bressieux (nine victories) routinely flew Hawk 75A-1 N°14 (X813) through to the end of May, claiming his first success in the aircraft on the 12th of that month when he downed a Bf 110C of 13.(Z)/LG 1. N°14 was

replaced by a Hawk 75A-3 on 16 June 1940, and the veteran aircraft was not flown to North Africa for further service.

5

Hawk 75A-1 N°5 (X804) '9' of GC II/5's 3rd *escadrille*, flown by Sgt Edouard Salès, Toul Croix-de-Metz, November 1939

GC II/5 was the second *Groupe de Chasse* to receive the Hawk 75, and it gained fame with the fighter during the autumn of 1939 – especially on 6 November, when nine pilots were engaged by Bf 109Ds in the so called '9-versus-27' dogfight. Future ace Sgt Edouard Salès, whose assigned aircraft at this time was Hawk 75A-1 N°5 (X804), claimed his first two victories during this action. Salès' fighter has the narrow rudder stripes that were applied to all Hawk 75A-1s during the summer of 1939 at Reims airfield.

6

Hawk 75A-3 N°202 of GC II/5, Headquarters, flown by Cdt Albert Petitjean-Roget, Toul Croix-de-Metz, June 1940

A handful of Hawk 75A-3s reached the frontline from 13 May 1940, with numbers increasing by month end. Amongst the aircraft issued to GC II/5's HQ on 17 May was N°202, which duly became Cdt Albert Petitjean-Roget's personal mount. Having claimed two of his five kills with it, Roget flew the fighter to North Africa in late June 1940.

7

Hawk 75A-1 N°64 (X863) '5' of GC II/4's 4th *escadrille*, flown by Adj Camille Plubeau, Reims, summer 1939

Another *Groupe de Chasse* that became famous during the Phoney War was GC II/4, which had received its first Hawk 75s in May 1939. Adj Camille Plubeau, who would ultimately become the unit's ranking ace, was issued with H-75A-1 N°64 (X963), although he failed to score any victories with it for the fighter was damaged in a flying accident on 11 September 1939. The 4th *escadrille*'s distinctive yellow unit emblems were overpainted within days of war being declared.

8

Hawk 75A-1 N°69 (X868) '1' of GC II/4's 3rd *escadrille*, flown by Lt Régis Guieu, Xaffévillers, autumn 1939

The 3rd *escadrille* emblem seen on the fuselage sides of Hawk 75A-1 N°69 was also removed shortly after 3 September 1939. This aircraft served as the personal mount of 'Red Devils'' CO Lt Régis Guieu until November 1939. N°69 was lightly damaged in combat on 24 September 1939, and Guieu was not flying it when he obtained the first of his seven confirmed victories on 30 September. In November, he received a six-gun Hawk 75A-2, although N°69 stayed with the *Groupe*. It was finally lost on 10 May 1940 when Sgt Georges Ballin took to his parachute after being badly wounded fighting Bf 110s over Epinal.

9

Hawk 75A-2 N°189 (U089) '7' of GC II/4's 3rd *escadrille*, flown by Sgt Chef Antoine Casenobe, Xaffévillers and Orconte, May 1940

Hawk 75A-2 N°189 was one of the few Curtiss fighters to feature personal markings, its nickname *Fanfan la Tulipe* being applied by its assigned pilot, Sgt Chef Antoine Casenobe (seven kills). He flew the aircraft from September 1939, having used it to claim one of the first aerial victories of the war on the 8th of that month. Casenobe enjoyed more success with the fighter during the Battle of France until it was damaged in early June 1940 whilst being flown by another pilot. N°189 was one of eight unserviceable Hawk 75s set on fire at Dun-sur-Auron on 17 June by GC II/4 prior to the airfield being abandoned to the Germans. Casenobe finished the Battle of France flying Hawk 75A-3 N°279.

10

Hawk 75A-2 N°115 (U015) '13' of GC I/4's 1st *escadrille*, flown by Sgt Jules Joire, Dunkerque (Nord) and Villacoublay, May 1940
Hawk 75A-2 N°115 was another Curtiss fighter to feature a nickname, bestowed upon it by Sgt Jules Joire (six victories). Far from the German frontier during the Phoney War, and then badly mauled during the Battle of France (nine pilots killed and twelve injured), GC I/4 produced only three aces in 1940. N°115 was flown by two of them, with Joire routinely sharing the aircraft with Adj Jean Hotellier (five victories). *FRANC* was lost on 25 May 1940 when Sgt Joire, wounded by return fire from a Do 17Z of II./KG 76, was forced to crash-land at Loeuilly.

11

Hawk 75A-4 N°8 '10' of GC II/5's 3rd *escadrille*, Casablanca, Morocco, July 1940
Very few Wright Cyclone engined Hawk 75s emerged from Bourges and Toulouse prior to the Armistice coming into effect. Indeed, the only action these aircraft saw was over Mers-El-Kébir in early July 1940. N°8 was amongst those machines to experience combat in North Africa with GC II/5's 3rd *escadrille*. Most of them would be taken out of service by the late summer of 1940 due to engine problems such as lubrication deficiency after just 30-50 flight hours.

12

Hawk 75A-3 N°259 '4' of GC I/5's 2nd *escadrille*, flown by Sous-Lt Georges Baptizet, Rabat, Morocco, late 1940
When GC II/4 was disbanded in North Africa in August 1940, most of the pilots from its 4th *escadrille* joined GC I/5's 2nd *escadrille*. Amongst them was nine-kill ace Sous-Lt Georges Baptizet, who had achieved his final three victories with N°259 in June 1940. The aircraft was adorned with GC 2/5's Vulture emblem, but also kept GC 4/4's *Petit Poucet* below the cockpit. N°259 would be destroyed on the ground by US Navy Wildcats from VGF-26 during the opening stages of Operation *Torch*, which commenced on 8 November 1942 .

13

Hawk 75A-2 N°173 (U073) '1' of GC II/5's 3rd *escadrille*, flown by Cne Hubert Monraisse, Casablanca, Morocco, September 1940
Having claimed six victories during the Battle of France, Cne Hubert Monraisse, CO of GC II/5's 3rd *escadrille*, flew Hawk 75A-2 N°173 to North Africa in late June 1940. He would claim his seventh, and last, success whilst flying this fighter

on 14 September 1940 when he shot down a Saro London from the RAF's No 202 Sqn off Casablanca.

14

Hawk 75A-3 N°319 '1' of GC I/4's 2nd *escadrille*, flown by Cne Louis Delfino, Dakar, Senegal, August 1942
On 14 July 1940, GC I/4 was despatched to Dakar, in Senegal, to defend its harbour, and the unit would remain here until 1943. Its pilots would gain a handful of victories against Allied aircraft during this period. Amongst the successful aviators was Cne Louis Delfino, CO of the 2nd *escadrille*, who scored his eighth kill on 12 August 1942 in N°319 when he downed a Wellington. He had previously claimed one victory with GC I/4 and six with GC II/9 (the latter unit flying Bloch MB.152s) during the Battle of France. Delfino would end the war as the CO of the *Normandie-Niemen* Régiment, having by then claimed 16 confirmed victories.

15

Hawk 75A-6 CUw-553/'White 3' of 1/LLv 32, flown by 2Lt Sakari Alapuro, Lappeenranta, September 1941
Alapuro flew with 1/LLv 32 from the beginning of the Continuation War, claiming his first kill (an I-153) in CUw-553 on 3 September 1941. With four victories to his credit, Alapuro was accepted into the officer cadet academy on 1 July 1942, where he stayed for a year. 1Lt Alapuro subsequently became the last CO of 3/HLeLv 32 following Capt Veikko Evinen's death on 25 June 1944. Three days later, Alapuro gained the distinction of being the last pilot to 'make ace' with HLeLv 32 when he downed a LaGG-3 without firing a shot – he simply outmanoeuvred the enemy fighter at low-level, causing it to crash. Alapuro had flown 211 missions by war's end.

16

Hawk 75A-3 CUw-563/'Yellow 3' of 2/LLv 32, flown by Capt Kullervo Lahtela, Lappeenranta, September 1941
Lahtela was an instructor at the Air Fighting School prior to becoming a fighter pilot at the end of the Winter War. He led 2/LLv 32 at the beginning of the Continuation War, took over 1/LLv 32 after Capt Paavo Berg's death on 1 November 1941 and was eventually made CO of 2/LeLv 34, flying Bf 109Gs, on 11 February 1943. At this point Lahtela's score stood at five and three shared victories, and with the Messerschmitt he added a further 4.5 kills to his total of ten and one shared during 187 missions. Lahtela returned to lead HLeLv 32 on 23 June 1944, and was promoted to major three weeks later.

17

Hawk 75A-2 CU-581/'Blue 1' of 3/HLeLv 32, flown by Capt Veikko Evinen, Nurmoila, February 1944
As a regular officer, Evinen served with LLv 32 from the beginning of the Continuation War. He claimed his unit's first two victories on 25 June 1941 by downing two DB-3 bombers in a D.XXI, followed by 1.5 with the Hawk 75. Evinen was posted to LeLv 34 on 26 March 1943, and flying the Bf 109G, he became an ace on 2 May 1943. Evinen returned to HLeLv 32 as CO of the 3rd Flight on 20 February 1944, and he was shot down by ground fire in CU-581 on 24 June. He succumbed to his wounds the following day. Evinen had flown 150+ missions by the time of his death.

18

Hawk 75A-4 CU-505/'Blue 5' of 2/HLeLv 32, flown by SSgt Väinö Virtanen, Nurmoila, March 1944

Virtanen was a reservist NCO who served throughout the Continuation War with LLv 32. He became an ace on 19 July 1942 after scoring a double in CU-552, and his eighth, and last, victory came on 5 May 1943 in CU-569. A veteran of 280+ missions, Virtanen was one of several pilots to fly sorties in CU-505 during the last year of the conflict. CU-505 had originally been powered by a Cyclone engine, but this had proven to be so unreliable that the aircraft was fitted with a Twin Wasp in March 1943.

19

Hawk 75A-2 CUw-551/'White 1' of 2/LeLv 32, flown by WO Eino Koskinen, Nurmoila, September 1942

Trained as a dive-bomber pilot, MSgt Koskinen served in the Winter War with LLv 10. He then became a test pilot, spending 15 months in this role prior to being posted as a warrant officer to LLv 32 on 20 June 1941. Koskinen remained with this unit until his untimely death in a road accident on 11 January 1945. He scored all but one of his 11 and 1 shared victories in the Hawk 75, CUw-551 being the aircraft he flew most frequently – he claimed 3.5 kills with the fighter on 5 September 1942. His single non-Hawk 75 victory came on 16 February 1944 when he used a captured LaGG-3 to down a Soviet LaGG-3! Koskinen flew some 350 missions.

20

Hawk 75A-6 CUw-558/'White 8' of 1/LeLv 32, flown by Sgt Niilo Erkinheimo, Nurmoila, August 1942

This aircraft was a real 'ace maker', as it was flown on numerous occasions by Alapuro, Hillo, Koskinen, Salminen and Virtanen, as well as Niilo Erkinheimo. Indeed, CUw-558 was credited with 17 victories, five of which were claimed by Erkinheimo. He had joined LLv 32 three months prior to the start of the Continuation War, and his score with the Hawk 75 stood at six and three shared kills by 25 March 1943, when he was transferred to Bf 109G-equipped LeLv 34. Erkinheimo made four more claims with the new fighter prior to his engine catching fire in flight on 16 November 1943, forcing him to ditch in the Gulf of Finland. He drowned in the cold water before a rescue boat could reach him. Erkinheimo had flown 180 missions by the time of his death.

21

Hawk 75A-3 CU-571/'Blue 1' of 3/LLv 32, flown by Capt Pentti Nurminen, Suulajärvi, March 1942

As leader of the 3rd Flight, Capt Nurminen flew this machine during the legendary aerial battle over Suursaari on 28 March 1942, claiming two victories. Nurminen was also an ex-dive-bomber pilot from LLv 10, serving with LLv 32 from 1 April 1941. His score stood at five and three shared victories when he was shot down by ground fire in CU-565 on 19 March 1943 and captured. Nurminen returned to Finland on 25 December 1944 during the Christmas PoW exchange. He had flown around 200 missions by the time he was captured.

22

Hawk 75A-2 CU-580/'Yellow 0' of 1/HLeLv 32, flown by 1Lt Jaakko Hillo, Nurmoila, October 1943

Hillo had been accepted into the officer cadet academy just prior to the start of the Continuation War, but was mobilised on 20 June 1941 and sent to LLv 32 before he could start his course. Flying as an NCO, he became an ace on 7 June 1942, and three weeks later went back to the academy and subsequently graduated as a first lieutenant. Hillo returned to LeLv 32 on 4 June 1943. He kept on scoring during 1944, and by the end of hostilities, his tally stood at eight and one shared destroyed from a total of 220 missions. His solitary victory in CU-580 came on 22 June 1944, when he shared in the destruction of an Il-2.

23

Mohawk IV 2511 of No 4 Sqn SAAF, flown by Lt H E N Wildsmith, Nakuru, Kenya, June 1941

The first SAAF unit to receive the Mohawk was No 4 Sqn when it formed in Kenya in mid 1941. It was working up prior to deploying to Egypt, and had a number of pilots who would find great success there. Among them was Lt Hugh Wildsmith, who made six claims, including four destroyed. He regularly flew 2511 (previously BS794), which was a presentation aircraft paid for by farmers from Louis Trichardt, hence it was named *NORTHERN TRANSVAAL*.

24

Mohawk IV 2514 of No 3 Sqn SAAF, flown by Capt J E Parsonson, Aisca, Ethiopia, September 1941

The only SAAF Mohawks to see action were those of No 3 Sqn based in East Africa, which flew ground attack missions against the Italians and intercepted the odd Vichy-French aircraft. The only pilot to claim an aeroplane destroyed, albeit on the ground, whilst flying a Mohawk in this theatre was Capt Jack Parsonson, who went on to become an ace. 2514 was one of the aircraft detached to the border of French Somaliland, and Parsonson was at the controls on 27 September 1941 when, at the end of a test flight, it suffered a minor accident.

25

P-36A 38-92 of the 47th PS/15th PG, flown by 2Lt Harry W Brown, Haleiwa Field, Hawaii, 7 December 1941

This P-36A was one of several based at Haleiwa Auxiliary Field for weapon qualification training when the Japanese attacked Pearl Harbor on 7 December 1941. This meant that it escaped the carnage wrought on USAAC fighters at Hickam, Bellows and Wheeler Fields. At 0830 hrs, 2Lt Harry Brown took off in 38-92 and quickly became embroiled with a pair of Japanese B5N 'Kate' torpedo-bombers, one of which he sent crashing into the sea in flames. He then flew through a large formation of B5Ns, one of which he engaged along with another P-36, and it was last seen limping away trailing smoke – this 'Kate' was later credited to him as destroyed too. Brown's feat on 7 December was all the more remarkable because his P-36 was armed with only a single 0.30-in machine gun due to a shortage of weapons in Hawaii!

26

Mohawk IV BJ546/OQ-O of No 5 Sqn, flown by Sgt C V Bargh, Akyab, Burma, 16-20 March 1942

After being evacuated from Burma for a few days in mid-March 1942, several Hurricane II pilots from No 67 Sqn were attached to No 5 Sqn to fly Mohawks in the defence of the Burmese port of Akyab. One such pilot was Sgt 'Ketchil' Bargh, who had achieved some success over Burma in the Buffalo, and who flew this particular aircraft. Although the Mohawk was finished in standard fighter colours, note that the stroke of the letter 'Q' in its unit code took the form of a curved native dagger, and a white wolf's head was painted on the engine cowling. Bargh soon returned to No 67 Sqn, while BJ546 was written off an accident in November.

27
Mohawk IV BS788/NA-A of No 146 Sqn, flown by Sqn Ldr M B Czernin, Dinjan, Assam, India, 23 April 1942
No 146 Sqn only received a handful of Mohawks, which the unit's Battle of Britain ace CO flew for the first time on 5 April when he performed a familiarisation flight. Later that same day Czernin scrambled in one, although he failed to make contact with the enemy. Manfred Czernin flew BS788 for the first time on 23 April when he sortied from Dinjan to Tezpur and back. By then all the Mohawks in the unit bore No 146 Sqn's 'NA' code letters, unusually applied in black. In early May BS788 was transferred to No 5 Sqn, who subsequently transferred it to No 155 Sqn. Therefore, it may be the only Mohawk to have served with all three units.

28
Mohawk IV 2529 of No 6 Sqn SAAF, flown by Maj M S Osler, Groutville, South Africa, 29 August 1942
Six-victory desert ace Maj 'Bennie' Osler took command of No 6 Sqn on 6 July 1942, his unit being the only Mohawk outfit to become operational in South Africa. The squadron was tasked with defending coastal areas from aerial attack, although warning of the only known incursion – a submarine-launched Japanese floatplane – came too late for the Mohawks to scramble. Osler in known to have flown 2529, which carried the unit's mauve/blue diamond marking, during the squadron's move to Cape Town on 29 August.

29
Mohawk IV BJ442/Y of No 155 Sqn, flown by Sqn Ldr D W A Stones, Alipore, India, 30 October 1942
Sqn Ldr 'Dimsie' Stones, who had become an ace over Malta, was the first CO of No 155 Sqn. Unfortunately, due to an altercation with a Provost Officer, he lost his command after leading the unit on its first mission – a long range strafing attack on the Japanese airfield at Shwebo, in central Burma on 30 October. Stones flew this aircraft, which carried no unit codes, on the mission. BJ442 remained with No 155 Sqn until it was withdrawn from service in September 1943.

30
Mohawk IV BS790/WPB of No 169 Wing, flown by Sqn Ldr W Pitt-Brown, Agartala, India, November-December 1942
No 169 Wing formed in October 1942 to control both Nos 5 and 155 Sqns, with the former unit's CO, Sqn Ldr Bill Pitt-Brown, being appointed as Wing Leader. He adopted this aircraft as his personal mount, and as was his privilege, adorned it with his initials. Pitt-Brown flew it regularly when leading his units, and he was at the controls on 10 November when, off Akyab, he was credited with the destruction of a

Ki-43 'Oscar'. Although this was his only aerial victory, Pitt-Brown was a consummate leader, and later headed up a Typhoon wing over Normandy in 1944.

31
Mohawk IV BJ439/V of No 5 Sqn, flown by Flg Off W J N Lee, Agartala, India, February-May 1943
Although he could not register a single confirmed victory, Flg Off John Lee was one of only two RAF pilots to make five *claims* with the Mohawk. BJ439 was his regular aircraft, and he is first known to have flown it on 3 February. He continued to regularly sortie in the fighter until the squadron was re-equipped with Hurricane IIs in July 1943. He was at the controls of BJ439 on 29 March 1943 when, in a desperate combat over the Arakan, he was credited with one Ki-43 probably destroyed and two others damaged, although he too was hit and wounded in the engagement. Sadly, Lee was killed later in the war, while his aircraft, which carried his personal marking, was eventually passed on to No 155 Sqn.

32
Mohawk IV BJ545/C of No 155 Sqn, flown by Sqn Ldr C G St D Jeffries, Imphal, India, November 1943
The only Commonwealth ace to be credited with an aerial victory in the the Mohawk, 'Porky' Jeffries was CO of No 155 Sqn for almost a year. During his last few weeks with the unit he regularly flew BJ545, and was in it on 2 November when he led a six-aircraft strafe on a Japanese camp in the Tauk area. This was in fact his final operational sortie with the squadron, as Jeffries handed over command soon afterwards. His aircraft, which carries the then current India Command pattern roundels, was scrapped soon after being withdrawn from service in early 1944.

Back Cover
Hawk 75A-2 N°107 (U007) of Etampes DAT flight, flown by Sous-Lt Jan Zumbach, Villacoublay, June 1940
Hawk H-75A-2 N°107 was assigned to GC I/4's 2nd *escadrille* from October 1939 through to May 1940. During this time it was the personal mount of Lt Jacques Tardy de Montravel, who was awarded a confirmed victory with it on 11 May 1940 when he downed an He 111P from KG 54. N°107 subsequently joined the Etampes DAT flight at Villacoublay in early June, where it was flown by future Polish ace Sous-Lt Jan Zumbach. He did not obtain any victories with it during the Battle of France, however, and N°107 was captured intact by the Germans and sold to Finland in 1941. Coded CUw-556, the Hawk 75 claimed 11 kills with the Finnish Air Force.

ACKNOWLEDGEMENTS

The authors wish to record their gratitude to the following former Hawk 75, P-36 and Mohawk pilots who have given of their time in answering queries and presenting accounts for inclusion within this volume – the late Lt Col A S Alaspuro, H Bishop, the late Lt Col A N Bremer, the late Gp Capt T A F Elsdon OBE DFC, W S Garnett DFC, J J Hillo, Wg Cdr G S Hogan, K K Karhila, the late Lt Col K Lahtela, the late R R Lawrence, the late Flt Lt J S Linn, Air Cdre W Pitt-Brown CBE DFC AFC and D R Wicks.

INDEX

References to illustrations are shown in **bold**. Plates are shown with page and caption locators in brackets.